GOD'S
WORD
*H*EALS

Derek PRINCE

WHITAKER
HOUSE

Publisher's Note: This book was compiled from the extensive archive of Derek Prince's unpublished materials and edited by the Derek Prince Ministries editorial team.

Unless otherwise noted, Scripture quotations are taken from the *New King James Version*, © 1979, 1980, 1982, 1984 by Thomas Nelson, Inc. Used by permission. All rights reserved. Scripture quotations marked (KJV) are taken from the King James Version of the Holy Bible. Scripture quotations marked (NASB) are taken from the *New American Standard Bible*®, NASB®, © 1960, 1962, 1963, 1971, 1972, 1973, 1975, 1977, 1988 by The Lockman Foundation. Used by permission. (www.Lockman.org) Scripture quotations marked (TLB) are taken from *The Living Bible*, © 1971. Used by permission of Tyndale House Publishers, Inc., Wheaton, Illinois 60189. All rights reserved. Scripture quotations marked (AMP) are taken from the *Amplified® Bible*, © 1954, 1958, 1962, 1964, 1965, 1987 by The Lockman Foundation. Used by permission. (www.Lockman.org).

Note: This book is not intended to provide medical advice or to take the place of medical advice and treatment from your personal physician. Neither the publisher nor the author's ministry takes any responsibility for any possible consequences from any action taken by any person reading or following the information in this book. If readers are taking prescription medications, they should consult with their physicians and not take themselves off prescribed medicines without the proper supervision of a physician. Always consult your physician or other qualified health care professional before undertaking any change in your physical regimen, whether fasting, diet, medications, or exercise.

GOD'S WORD HEALS

ISBN: 978-1-60374-210-8
Printed in the United States of America
© 2010 by Derek Prince Ministries, International

Derek Prince Ministries
P.O. Box 19501
Charlotte, North Carolina 28219
www.derekprince.org

Whitaker House
1030 Hunt Valley Circle
New Kensington, PA 15068
www.whitakerhouse.com

Library of Congress Cataloging-in-Publication Data

Prince, Derek.
God's Word heals / by Derek Prince.
    p. cm.
    ISBN 978-1-60374-210-8 (trade pbk. : alk. paper) 1. Spiritual healing—Christianity. I. Title.
BT732.5.P75 2010
234'.131—dc22

                                            2009053160

3 4 5 6 7 8 9 10 11 12 **UJ** 19 18 17 16 15 14 13 12

Contents

Chapter One

Jesus, Our Healer

The purpose of this book is to help anyone who needs to be healed—and that would include most of us. Much of what I share in these pages has to do with physical healing, with a chapter on deliverance and renewal of the mind, and my desire is that you will experience healing yourself.

HEALING IS AN IMPORTANT PART OF THE GOSPEL

In addition to spiritual rebirth, physical healing is an important part of the gospel message. How can we be sure of this? Jesus came to earth to demonstrate the will of God. He said,

> *I have come down from heaven, not to do My own will, but the will of Him who sent Me.*
> (John 6:38 NASB)

> *The words that I speak to you I do not speak on My own authority; but the Father who dwells in Me does the works.* (John 14:10)

*Whatever I speak, just as the Father has told
Me, so I speak.*   (John 12:50)

Jesus summed it up when He said, *"He who has
seen Me has seen the Father"* (John 14:9). If you
want to know what God the Father is like and what
His will is, Jesus directs you to look at Him and
His earthly ministry.

In the book of Acts, the apostle Peter presented the earthly ministry of Jesus in one beautiful
thought, in one succinct verse:

> *God anointed Jesus of Nazareth with the Holy
> Spirit and with power,* **who went about do-
> ing good and healing** *all who were oppressed
> by the devil.*   (Acts 10:38, emphasis added)

All three persons of the Godhead are included
in the above verse. God the Father anointed Jesus
the Son with the Holy Spirit. Colossians 2:9 says,
"For in [Jesus] *dwells all the fullness of the Godhead bodily."* What was the result of Jesus being
present on earth? He *"went about doing good and
healing all who were oppressed by the devil."* Healing is attributed to Jesus; sickness and oppression,
to the devil. I like the fact that the Bible makes this
truth so clear and simple.

5

JESUS BROUGHT RIGHTEOUSNESS AND HEALING

In the fourth chapter of Malachi, we read, *"But to you who fear My name The Sun of Righteousness shall arise with healing in His wings"* (verse 2). I believe this is a prophecy of the last days because, as you read further along in that chapter, it leads right up to the climax of the age. And I believe this prophecy is being fulfilled now. *"To you who fear My name, The Sun of Righteousness shall arise with healing in His wings."* Jesus Christ, risen from the dead, is The Sun of Righteousness. In the natural world, the sun is the only source of light to our planet. In the spiritual world, Jesus is the only source of light to us. What does spiritual light bring? Righteousness and healing. Jesus came to bring deliverance from sin (righteousness), and deliverance from sickness (healing).

> **In the natural world, the sun is the only source of light to our planet. In the spiritual world, Jesus is the only source of light to us.**

The works of darkness are the opposite of the works of light. What is the opposite of righteousness?

Sin. What is the opposite of healing? Sickness. These facts are very clear. It is important that we keep them in mind as we progress through this book.

———— ❦ ————

WHY AREN'T SOME PEOPLE HEALED?

———— ❦ ————

Before exploring the nature of healing, we must address the question of why some people don't seem to be healed. Deuteronomy 29:29 says, *"The secret things belong to the LORD our God."* They are His business. The verse goes on to say, *"Those things which are revealed belong to us and to our children forever, that we may do all the words of this law."*

As far as I'm concerned, the reason some people don't get healed is a secret known only to God. Frankly, it is not my business to know God's business. *"The secret things belong to the LORD."* However, everything that is revealed in the Scriptures belongs to us and to our children, so that we may act on it. Let us discover, therefore, what is revealed in the Scriptures about healing.

The great saintly woman, Corrie ten Boom, used to quote this saying: "KISS: Keep it simple, stupid!" That is my aim—to keep the issue of healing simple.

GETTING YOU INVOLVED

I want to encourage you to get personally involved in this matter of healing. My concept of healing ministry is that members of the body of Christ should come together to minister healing to other members of the body. What I share in the following chapters will lead you step-by-step into an understanding of how to receive your own healing and how to minister healing to others.

My good friend Bob Mumford once said that he believed the world was beginning to look to the church and expect something from it. I have always felt it ought to be that way. For too many years, the world has taken absolutely no notice of the church. But I believe God intends for that to be different than it has been. The world is beginning to take note of what we are doing. It is not happening too soon, by any means.

What will cause the world to notice the church will not be political power. It will be spiritual power—including the manifestation of healing. It is very important that we bear that in mind.

A PRAYER OF INVOLVEMENT IN HEALING

As a first step in your understanding of healing, and also your involvement in active healing ministry, I want you to repeat a powerful prayer that is found in Acts 4. This prayer was a collective petition voiced by the early disciples.

Let me give you some background to this petition. For the first time since Jesus had returned to heaven after His resurrection, the apostles had run head-on into opposition. The political and religious leaders had forbidden them to preach in the name of Jesus any longer. It is amazing to see that, sometimes, the opposition is more discerning than God's people are. They realized that if the apostles were forced to take the name of Jesus out of their ministry, the power would go out of it as well.

The reason? Every promise of God the Father is valid only in the name of Jesus. *"For all the promises of God in Him are Yes, and in Him Amen, to the glory of God"* (2 Corinthians 1:20). I'm sure Satan planted this thought in the minds of those officials: *We will tell them not to speak anymore in the name of Jesus.* (See Acts 4:17.)

Confronted by this situation, the leaders of the early church went back to their group, which probably still met in the Upper Room. The leaders called the early disciples together and said, "We have to pray." When they all came together, they prayed a united prayer by the inspiration of the Holy Spirit. Significantly, the Holy Spirit caused that prayer to be recorded in Scripture, which leads me to believe that it must be a good model for us, and that it is not out-of-date.

I want you to read these two verses of Acts 4, not just as a Scripture reading, but also as a prayer for you to get involved with the work of God in your life and in the world. Please pray this prayer:

> *Now, Lord, look on their threats, and grant to Your servants that with all boldness they may speak Your word, by stretching out Your hand to heal, and that signs and wonders may be done through the name of Your holy Servant Jesus.* (Acts 4:29–30)

NOW YOU ARE INVOLVED!

You have just prayed a very specific prayer. It is a life-changing prayer. It changed the lives of the early disciples, who petitioned, "Lord, we need You to come

10

to our help. We are confronted with opposition; there must be a breakthrough." They specifically asked, "Lord, will You stretch forth Your hand to heal? And will You grant signs and wonders to be done in the name of Jesus?"

It takes a certain amount of courage to pray that kind of prayer—and mean it. Some Christians pray such vague prayers that they wouldn't know if God had really answered them or not! Those prayers are safe, but they are useless. The type of prayer that God answers is a commitment. It is something specific that you will know whether or not He has answered. The disciples' prayer was specific, and I am asking you to pray it to God again as you read it once more.

Now, Lord, look on their threats, and grant to Your servants that with all boldness they may speak Your word, by stretching out Your hand to heal, and that signs and wonders may be done through the name of Your holy Servant Jesus. (Acts 4:29–30)

Now, you have prayed it. From this moment on, your life will be different.

Chapter Two

God Saves, Heals, and Delivers

As I continue to lay the scriptural foundation for healing, I want to focus on the first half of Psalm 107, because it is so helpful to our understanding of God's provision for us in this way. I hope you will take in its truths and be ready to act on them. Let's begin by reading the first seventeen verses of this psalm.

Oh, give thanks unto the LORD, for He is good! For His mercy endures forever. Let the redeemed of the LORD say so, whom He has redeemed from the hand of the enemy, and gathered out of the lands, from the east and from the west, from the north and from the south. They wandered in the wilderness in a desolate way; they found no city to dwell in. Hungry and thirsty, their soul fainted in them. Then they cried out to the LORD in their trouble, and He delivered them out of their distresses. And He led them forth by the right way, that they might go to a city for a dwelling place. Oh, that men would give thanks to the LORD for His goodness, and for

*His wonderful works to the children of men!
For He satisfies the longing soul, and fills the
hungry soul with goodness. Those who sat in
darkness and in the shadow of death, bound
in affliction and irons; because they rebelled
against the words of God, and despised the
counsel of the Most High, therefore He brought
down their heart with labor; they fell down,
and there was none to help. Then they cried
out to the LORD in their trouble, and He saved
them out of their distresses. He brought them
out of darkness and the shadow of death, and
broke their chains in pieces. Oh, that men
would give thanks to the LORD for His goodness, and for His wonderful works to the children of men! For He has broken the gates of
bronze, and cut the bars of iron in two. Fools,
because of their transgression, and because of
their iniquities, were afflicted.*

(Psalm 107:1–17)

MAN IS RESPONSIBLE FOR HIS CONDITION

Psalm 107 tells it like it is, doesn't it? You will
notice that all through this psalm, man is shown
to be responsible for his own sorry situation. Every

13

time the Bible, the Word of God, places the responsibility on man for his foolishness, his disobedience,
his rebellion, and his rejection of God's Word and
counsel, it is putting the responsibility right where
it belongs—on us. We can't try to shift it back onto
God.

Let's continue reading Psalm 107, starting with
the verse with which we left off:

*Fools, because of their transgression, and be-
cause of their iniquities, were afflicted. Their
soul abhorred all manner of food, and they
drew near to the gates of death.*

(verses 17–18)

In other words, their condition was terminal.
Their case was hopeless. The doctor couldn't do
anything to help them. They had lost all appetite
and couldn't take in any nourishment. They were
right at death's door, so they were just waiting to
die.

I like the next verse very much. It says, *"Then
they cried out to the LORD"* (Psalm 107:19). Some
people wait until the last minute before praying,
don't they? When you are at death's door, it is indeed the very last moment when you have an opportunity to pray. *"Then they cried out to the LORD
in their trouble, and He saved them out of their distresses"* (verse 19).

HOW GOD RESPONDS TO MAN'S DESPERATE CONDITION

What does the Lord send to answer our desperate cries for help?

He sent His word and healed them, and delivered them from their destructions. Oh, that men would give thanks to the LORD for His goodness, and for His wonderful works to the children of men! Let them sacrifice the sacrifices of thanksgiving, and declare His works with rejoicing.

(Psalm 107:20–22)

God sends His Word to answer our need. Notice that, in sending His Word, He does three major things:

*Then they cried out to the LORD in their trouble, and He **saved** them out of their distresses. He sent His word and **healed** them, and **delivered** them from their destructions.*

(verses 19–20, emphasis added)

What are the three things God does? He saves, He heals, and He delivers. By what means does He do these things? By His Word.

15

THE BASIS FOR RECEIVING IS THE WORD OF GOD

Let me state very clearly that the basis for receiving salvation, healing, or deliverance is the Word of God. Never seek to bypass God's Word to get results. Likewise, the basis for healing ministry is the Word of God. When Jesus gave instructions to His twelve disciples before sending them out to minister, He began by saying, *"As you go, preach"* (Matthew 10:7). Then, He said, *"Heal the sick, cleanse the lepers, raise the dead, cast out demons"* (verse 8). It is the Word that brings the healing, the cleansing, the raising of the dead, and the casting out of demons. Everything centers on the Word of God.

> **It is the Word that brings the healing, the cleansing, the raising of the dead, and the casting out of demons.**

Before anyone attempts to minister healing, it is essential that he understand what God's Word, the Bible, says about it. When hearing teaching on healing, some people might think, *I wish he would stop teaching and get to praying.* That is a counterproductive attitude. James 1:21 says, *"Receive with meekness the implanted* [*"engrafted"* KJV] *word, which is able to save your souls."* That *"word"* is not merely able to save your soul, but it is also able to heal your body— if you will receive the word with meekness, and if you will open your heart to the Lord. If you will allow God's Word to be combined with faith inside you, it will accomplish God's purposes.

A KEY VERSE FOR UNDERSTANDING HEALING

An especially important verse for building our scriptural foundation for healing is 1 Peter 2:24. Peter wrote,

> [Christ] *Himself bore our sins in His own body on the tree, that we, having died to sins, might live for righteousness; by whose stripes* [*"wounds"* NASB] *you were healed.*

The Greek word translated *"healed"* in this verse is the word that specifically means physical healing. It is the word from which the Greek word for doctor is derived.

I had a dynamic experience with this verse many years ago when I was a missionary in Kenya, East Africa. I had gone every day for a week to preach to a congregation of about five hundred Africans. One day, I decided to preach on 1 Peter 2:24 because, to me, it is the heart and core of the gospel message. I planned to preach on the wonderful transaction and transformation that comes when we die to sin and come alive to righteousness. I wanted to focus on how death must precede life, and that you cannot live until you die. That is God's order: *"That we, having died to sins, might live for righteousness."* To me, that truth is profound.

Yet, as I was driving my car to this meeting, the thought came to me, *Probably 80 percent of the people you are about to preach to are illiterate. They can't read or write. How can you expect them to understand these profound truths?* I began to question whether I was going to present the right message. But, as I drove on, it was as though the Holy Spirit said to me, *Just go through that verse in your mind in the King James Version. Count the number of words in that verse, and see how many words have only one syllable.* I did just that, and I found that there are thirty words in the verse: one word of three syllables, four words of two syllables, and twenty-five words of one syllable. Feel free to check it for yourself. Yet I do not know any statement in the English language that is more profound than that verse. God seemed to say to me, *These are just the words those people understand. That is right where they live.*

Often, the most profound concepts are best expressed in the simplest terms. In fact, I believe that if I cannot convey a truth simply, I have not understood it clearly myself. I would always work at it until I could, and sometimes it took me years to do so. But we must be able to express a truth so simply that a child of twelve can easily understand it. That has been my aim in preaching. It may not be everybody's aim, but it has been my aim. I made it my aim to say things so simply and so obviously that nobody would waste his time disagreeing with them.

PERSEVERANCE IN HEALING

I learned something profound about healing in those meetings in Kenya. As I said, I preached there for seven successive days. Every day, at the end of my message, I said, "How many of you would like me to pray for your healing?" And, every day, quite a large number of people stood up for me to pray for their healing. Every day, a blind woman was led by the hand to the meeting by a little boy. And, every day, for six days, when I said, "Who wants to stand and receive prayer for healing?" she stood up. I prayed, but she remained blind.

On the seventh day, which was Sunday, so many people attended the meeting that they all couldn't fit

19

in the building. So we met on the hillside in the open air. I did exactly the same thing I had done inside the building where we had met. I preached, and, at the end, I said, "How many people want me to pray for their healing?" A great number stood up; the blind woman stood up with them, for the seventh day in succession. I closed my eyes, prayed for their healing, paused a moment, and then opened my eyes. Do you know what I saw? The blind woman was walking forward to show everybody that she had received her sight!

That was a rather important lesson to me. That woman didn't intend to give up. After six times, nothing had happened, but she didn't say, "It doesn't work!" She just stood up the seventh time. Sometimes, faith demands persistence.

OBEDIENCE IN HEALING

Do you remember the Old Testament account of Naaman? (See 2 Kings 5:1–14.) He was the commander of the army of the king of Syria, but he was also a leper. He heard through his slave girl, an Israelite, that there was a prophet in Israel who could heal him. Naaman then went to the king of Israel with a letter from the king of Syria, which said, in effect, "Heal

Naaman of his leprosy." The king of Israel became quite upset at this and said, "Who does he think I am, to heal people?" Elisha the prophet heard about the king of Israel's reaction, and he sent a message to the king, saying, "Send him to me. Let him know there is a prophet in Israel."

So, Naaman went to Elisha's door. Like most wealthy and influential people, he thought he could come to God in a big way that would impress Him. He came with his chariot, with his horses, with silver, with gold, with ten changes of clothing, and with many servants. He had an idea in his mind of what a miraculous healing would look like: *Elisha will come out and do something dramatic. He will wave his hand over me, and I'll be healed.* But the Holy Spirit knows just how and where to reach people. And the Holy Spirit instructed Elisha, in essence, *Don't go out and pray for him. Don't show yourself too interested in him. Don't let him impress you with his wealth and his social position. Just send a message: "Go and wash in the Jordan seven times, and you will be healed."*

Have you ever seen the river Jordan? Well, I was baptized in it on August 24, 1942. It is not a beautiful, romantic river. It is a muddy stream. When I stood in it, I had to do all I could to prevent my feet from slipping on the mud at the bottom.

Naaman looked at the Jordan and said, "That river? That muddy stream? Why, in my country, we have beautiful rivers that flow down from the mountains, pure and clear. Are not Abanah and Pharpar, the rivers of Damascus, better than all the rivers of Israel?" Naaman got angry and was about to stomp away in a rage. But one of his servants said to him, "My father, if the prophet had told you to do something great, wouldn't you have done it? How much more, then, when he says to you, 'Wash and be clean'?" Fortunately, Naaman was wise enough to get the message. So, he stripped. That also must have been a test of his humility, because he had to display his leprous flesh. He went down into the river and dipped himself in it seven times.

> **It is God's responsibility to do His part of the work. But if you don't obey, you have no claim on God.**

It is very clear from this passage in 2 Kings that, after six dips, there was no change whatever in Naaman's condition. How easy it would have been for him to say, "It doesn't work!" But he dipped the seventh time and came up healed.

God demands obedience, and it is your responsibility to obey. Certainly, it is God's responsibility to do His part of the work. But if you don't obey, you have no claim on God.

THE AMAZING EXCHANGE

Let's return to the key verse we looked at earlier:

[Christ] *Himself bore our sins in His own body on the tree, that we, having died to sins, might live for righteousness—by whose stripes ["wounds" NASB] you were healed.*

(1 Peter 2:24)

Christ bearing our sins speaks of God's provision for forgiveness and deliverance from the power of sin. Jesus bore our sins in His own body on the cross. To what purpose? *"That we, having died to sins"*—or, having been set free from the slavery of sin—*"might live for righteousness."*

The first part of the verse highlights the spiritual aspect of what Christ did on the cross. The second part reveals the physical provision of God: *"By whose stripes you were healed."* It's a very remarkable fact: when the Bible speaks about healing, referring to the atoning sacrifice of Christ in the Bible, it never uses the future tense.

By Christ's physical wounds, physical healing was provided for us.

23

In the book of Isaiah, which was written seven hundred years before Christ, we read,

> *Surely He has borne our griefs* [the correct translation is "sickness"] *and carried our sorrows* [the correct translation is "pain"];...*and by His stripes* ["*wounds*" KJV] *we are healed.*
>
> (Isaiah 53:4–5)

Notice that the future tense is not used. It is not "we will be healed" but *"we are healed."* What the Hebrew actually says is difficult to translate, but I'll give you a loose translation: "With His wounds, it was healed to us." The phrase is an impersonal past tense. In other words, by His physical wounds, physical healing was provided for us. Jesus took the evil so that we, in return, might receive the good. *"The LORD has laid on Him the iniquity of us all"* (Isaiah 53:6). Rebellion and all its evil consequences came upon Jesus as He hung on the cross. His soul was made sin. His body was made sickness. He was made a curse. He died. All this He did so that we, in return, might receive the corresponding good.

In place of sin, God offers us righteousness.

In place of sickness, God offers us health.

In place of the curse, God offers the blessing.

In place of death, God offers life.

It was an act of exchange. All the evil due to the rebellious human race came upon Jesus, the sinless Son of God, so that all the good that was due to Jesus by eternal right might be available to the whole human race. This is the meaning of the cross.

APPROPRIATE THE HEALING ALREADY PROVIDED

In 1 Peter 2:24, Peter quoted Isaiah some years after the death and resurrection of Jesus. Notice, again, that he put it in the past tense: *"By whose stripes* [*"wounds"* NASB] *you were healed."* As far as the Lord is concerned, your healing is already provided.

You might still ask, "How can I know if it's the will of God to heal me?" My answer is, "If you are a believer in Jesus Christ, a child of God through faith in Jesus, you are not phrasing the question right. The correct question is not, 'Is it God's will to heal me?' Rather, it is, 'How may I appropriate the healing that God has already provided for me?'"

I believe that healing has already been provided through Christ. I believe it when I'm well, and I believe it when I'm sick. Those are two different situations. It is one thing to believe in divine healing when you are well. That's good, but it is not difficult to believe when you are healthy. It is much more important to believe in divine healing when you are sick. That is what I discovered. When I was in the service during World War II, I lay in a hospital bed in Egypt for one full year while the doctors attempted unsuccessfully to heal me of chronic eczema, a skin condition. Then, I got out of hospital, and God healed me, because I came to believe what He said in His Word about healing. I am not preaching a theory that I have not applied in practice. God our Father has provided healing for His children.

My personal conviction is that the question of God's will concerning healing has already been settled. I don't want to dispute with anybody. As far as I'm concerned, "By His wounds, we were healed." The provision has been made.

In the next chapter, we will look more closely at the nature of faith—a very important ingredient for all types of healing.

Chapter Three

What Kind of Faith Do We Need for Healing?

I want to begin this chapter by focusing on four basic truths about the nature of faith, because faith is absolutely essential to the matter of healing. Though there is much talk about faith in Christian circles, most Christians are very confused as to its real nature.

FOUR TRUTHS ABOUT THE NATURE OF FAITH

Faith Is Individual

The first two truths are found in Habakkuk 2:4: *"The just ["righteous" NASB] shall live by his faith."* This verse contains certain simple but vital facts. First of all, faith is individual. The righteous man lives by his own faith. He doesn't live by somebody else's faith.

You cannot rely on your husband's faith, your wife's faith, your parents' faith, or your pastor's faith. You have to live by *your* faith. You have to face this responsibility squarely. God will not accept anybody else's faith as a permanent substitute for yours. He may do so temporarily, but He expects you to acquire and live by your own, personal faith.

Living by Faith Is All-Inclusive

Second, we need to see how all-inclusive this statement is: *"The just shall live by his faith"* (Habakkuk 2:4). Living includes everything: breathing, thinking, eating, talking, walking, working, praying, and all the rest. The only basis acceptable to God for any kind of activity is the faith basis. Romans 14:23 says, *"Whatever is not from faith is sin."* It doesn't matter if it is a religious activity. If it is not based on faith, it is sinful. There is only one basis on which God will accept any activity. *"Without faith it is impossible* [notice that: *impossible*] *to please* [God]" (Hebrews 11:6). Many people are trying hard to please God without faith, but it cannot be done.

The Life of Faith Is Progressive

Third, we need to see that the life of faith is progressive. It is not static. It is not a condition. Misunderstanding this aspect of faith is the greatest snare of the majority of Christians. They often feel they can come to a place where they are able to say, "This is it. I've experienced this, and I've experienced that. I know this, and I know that. I've *arrived.*" Yet this is not what the Bible teaches.

Life is something that progresses; it never stands still. The apostle Paul said to the men of Athens: *"In Him we live and move and have our being"* (Acts 17:28). One thing is sure: if you live, you move. When you cease to move altogether, you're dead. This is true in the natural, and it's also true in the spiritual.

Job 17:9 says, *"The righteous will hold to his way, and he who has clean hands will be stronger and stronger."* The righteous man is moving forward and getting stronger all the time. If you are not moving forward and getting stronger all the time, you are not living the life of righteousness by faith.

Proverbs 4:18 says, *"The path of the just* ["righteous" NASB] *is like the shining sun, that shines ever brighter unto the perfect day."* If you are in the way of righteousness, it is a pathway, and the light is getting brighter every day. You should stop from time to time to check on your spiritual condition. Is

> **If you are in the way of righteousness, it is a pathway, and the light is getting brighter every day.**

the light brighter today than it was yesterday? Is it brighter now than it was at this time a year ago? If not, you are in spiritual danger. You had better stop and analyze where you have gotten off the pathway and where you may be missing God.

The Only Basis for Faith Is God's Word

The fourth thing we need to see about faith is that it has only one basis. It is based solely, exclusively, on the Bible, the Word of God. Hebrews 11:1 tells us, *"Faith is the substance of things hoped for, the evidence of things not seen."* Over many years of teaching, I have repeatedly pointed out that the biblical concepts of *faith* (belief; a sure persuasion or conviction of the truth of God's Word) and *hope* (confident expectation of good in the future) are entirely distinct.

The great majority of Christians who seek healing seek it only in hope, but not also in faith, so they do not receive it. In other words, they may want to receive, but they haven't made their requests relying on the basis and qualifications for healing that are provided in God's Word. I have to be brutally frank about this. They are seeking healing on the basis of hope, but they have omitted the prerequisite of faith. They may not even know the difference between the two. Yet, again, what God has promised of faith, He has not made available to hope apart from faith. Let us therefore examine more closely the basic differences between faith and hope.

How can we more fully understand the crucial differences between faith and hope? First Thessalonians 5:8 talks about *"putting on the breastplate of faith and love* [indicating the region of the heart], *and as a helmet the hope of salvation* [indicating the region of the mind]."

30

THE CRUCIAL DIFFERENCES BETWEEN FAITH AND HOPE

First of all, then, faith is in the heart, while hope is in the mind. Second, faith is now and not in the future. Hope, on the other hand, is for the future—it is being confident that something will happen in the future. As Paul wrote, *"Hope that is seen is not hope; for why does one still hope for what he sees? But if we hope for what we do not see, we eagerly wait for it with perseverance"* (Romans 8:24–25).

Both faith and hope are valid and necessary in Christian experience. Paul wrote, *"Now abide faith, hope, love"* (1 Corinthians 13:13). Then, he concluded, *"The greatest of these is love"* (verse 13). But notice that faith and hope are quite distinct.

> **Faith is now, while hope is for the future.**

Faith is the substance, here and now in your heart, of things that you are hoping for in the future. It is a sure persuasion and unalterable conviction concerning the reality of things not seen, and those unseen things are what God says in His Word. Jesus said,

> *Have faith in God. For assuredly, I say to you, whoever says to this mountain, "Be removed and be cast into the sea," and does not doubt in*

31

his heart, but believes that those things he says will be done, he will have whatever he says. Therefore I say to you, whatever things you ask when you pray, believe that you receive them, and you will have them. (Mark 11:22–24)

Having faith in what God has said in His Word is the only kind of response acceptable to Him. Hebrews 11:3 says, *"By faith we understand that the worlds* [universe] *were framed* [brought into being, fitted together, constructed] *by the word of God, so that things which are seen were not made of things which are visible."* In other words, behind all physical, material life—everything that we know in the natural realm—there is the unseen, invisible, eternal, unchanging reality of God's Word.

Interestingly enough, modern physics is basically in agreement with this conclusion. In its own particular sphere and in its own terminology, it would say that *"things which are seen* [like your chair or your body] *were not made of things which are visible."* Matter is made up of material that is invisible to the naked eye—tiny little atoms, moving with tremendous speed, separated from one another by relatively enormous spaces, and describable only in terms of a mathematical equation. The basic reality cannot be seen.

We exercise faith in a number of realms. You may have faith in your doctor or faith in a particular politician. You have faith in the highway department. For example, when you are driving your car, you don't stop every time you get to the top of a hill to see if the road continues on the other side. You have complete faith in the highway department that the road doesn't end suddenly. That faith is perfectly valid in its realm.

However, in the Bible, faith always refers to faith in God and in His Word. In addition, there is no other basis, no other source, no other means by which you can *receive* faith than by His Word. Romans 10:17 says, *"So then faith comes by hearing, and hearing by the word of God."* As you hear, as you listen with complete attention, as you focus your whole mind, as you open your whole being to the Word of God, then faith comes. That is good news. Faith comes!

> **As you open your whole being to the Word of God, then faith comes.**

FAITH COMES

I mentioned in the previous chapter that I spent a year in a hospital in Egypt in 1942–43 because of a chronic skin condition that the doctors couldn't cure. As I lay month after month in my hospital bed, I realized that if I had faith, God could heal me. However, it was always a huge letdown to me that I didn't have faith. What could I do? I can tell you that I know what the "Slough of Despond" is like, as described by John Bunyan in *The Pilgrim's Progress*—the dark, lonely valley of despair. I was in my own slough of despond for weeks and months. But, one day, into that darkness came a bright ray of light that showed me the way out. It was Romans 10:17: *"So then faith comes."* I realized that if I didn't have faith, I could get it. And I got it. No matter where you are or what your situation is as you read this book, if you want faith, if you are determined to have it, if you meet God's conditions, if you will be desperate for it, you can get it.

THE NEED FOR DESPERATION

We do not have enough desperation in the church today. David Wilkerson, founder of Teen Challenge, has said to many drug addicts to whom he has ministered, "You can be delivered if you're desperate." This is true in every realm of deliverance. It is true for the person who needs deliverance from fear, depression, hatred, or resentment. Whatever it may be, if you are desperate, you can be delivered from it.

On one occasion, I took pity on a woman in a deliverance service in Arlington, Virginia. I saw her standing to the side looking distinctly unhappy. In fact, she looked lost. So, I walked up to her and said, "Can I help you?" She said, "Oh, yes! I have resentment and despair and hatred." I started to pray with her, and I really did my best. I put everything I had into the prayer, but there was no response. I said, "Listen, your problem is that you are expecting me to be desperate for you, and I can't do it." After a moment of silence, she replied, "The trouble is my dignity," to which I responded, "I thought it was that all along." Then, I said to her, "When you've made up your mind about that, I'll come back and pray for you." As far as I know, she didn't make up her mind about her dignity issue, nor did she ask me to come back and pray for her. She did not have the needed desperation.

An Example of Great, Desperate Faith

Think of the incident in Matthew 15 when the Syro-Phoenician woman came to Jesus for the healing and deliverance of her daughter, who was under the oppression and torment of an evil spirit. That woman was not an Israelite. That meant that she had no covenantal relationship with God. She had no claim on Jesus. You have to understand this fact to appreciate the context of her conversation with Jesus. She was outside the covenants of God and was therefore unclean. And Jesus used very uncomplimentary language in speaking to her. He said, *"It is not good to take the children's bread and throw it to the little dogs"* (Matthew 15:26).

She knew full well what He was calling her. If calling someone a dog is an insulting statement in the Western world, it is ten times more insulting in the Middle East, because dogs are not favored animals there. She didn't argue. She gave Him an amazing response: "True, Lord. I won't dispute the point. *'Yet even the little dogs eat the crumbs which fall from their masters' table'"* (verse 27). And Jesus said, *"O woman, great is your faith! Let it be to you as you desire"* (verse 28).

> **Healing belongs to the children of God. It is their basic, staple diet.**

In my judgment, no king, emperor, or president ever pinned a medal on anybody's chest that was worth as much as Jesus' response to her. *"O woman, great is your faith! Let it be to you as you desire."* He was saying, "Please help yourself. Take it. It's yours."

Did you notice what Jesus said about healing? He referred to it as *"the children's bread."* In other words, it belongs to the children of God. It is their basic, staple diet that is placed on the table every day. But, He said, "It isn't right to take that bread and throw it to the dogs." She answered, "Lord, I don't need a loaf. I don't even need a slice. All I need is a crumb.

That will be enough for my daughter's healing." No wonder Jesus said, *"O woman, great is your faith!"* Wouldn't you like to have faith like that?

Great Faith and Great Humility Go Together

Let's look at another aspect of faith for healing. There are two people in the New Testament who were praised by Jesus for their great faith. Each of them was a Gentile. One of them was this Syro-Phoenician woman, and the other was a Roman centurion, about whom Jesus said, *"Assuredly, I say to you, I have not found such great faith, not even in Israel!"* (Matthew 8:10).

Besides faith, these two people had at least one other characteristic in common—humility. The centurion said, *"Lord, I am not worthy that You should come under my roof"* (Matthew 8:8). The Syro-Phoenician woman said, in effect, "Lord, I'm just a dog, but all I need is a crumb." Great faith and great humility go together. The Bible says that *"boasting...is excluded"* (Romans 3:27). By what law is it excluded? *"The law of faith"* (verse 27). I have learned by experience that people who boast about how much faith they have actually don't have it. And they don't get what they say they have faith for. But the Lord meets those who come to Him in humility.

DARKNESS DISPELLED BY LIGHT

One requirement God ultimately demands of you is single-heartedness—having a "single eye." Jesus said, *"If therefore thine eye be single, thy whole body shall be full of light"* (Matthew 6:22 KJV), having no path dark. There is no room for sickness anywhere in your body when your whole body is filled with light.

Sickness is a work of darkness. But the scriptural counter to that is in this verse: *"But to you who fear My name The Sun of Righteousness shall arise with healing in His wings"* (Malachi 4:2). As I wrote in chapter one, *"The Sun of Righteousness"* is Jesus Christ, risen from the dead.

Remember the properties of the natural sun and the spiritual Sun that we discussed? In the natural realm, the sun is the only source of light and warmth in our area of the universe. In like manner, Jesus Christ, as The Sun of Righteousness, is the only source of true, spiritual light to us. He said, *"I am the light of the world"* (John 8:12). What does His light produce? Righteousness and healing: *"The Sun of Righteousness...with healing in His wings."*

What is the opposite of light? Darkness. What are the opposites of righteousness and healing? Sin and

WHAT KIND OF FAITH DO WE NEED FOR HEALING?

sickness. What are the works of darkness? Sin and sickness. Let's be clear about this. It is foolish for you to seek healing from sickness if you think that your sickness is a blessing placed upon you by God. Don't ask for prayer for healing with that attitude. Why would anyone want to help you to get rid of a blessing that God has placed upon you? You don't want that person to be fighting against God on your behalf, do you? If it's a blessing, cultivate it and hold on to it—but be consistent. Don't call it a blessing in church and go to a doctor on Monday morning and ask him to remove your "blessing." That just doesn't make sense. Be honest. Face facts. Faith is based on the written Word of God, the Bible. That is its only basis.

Let me say one thing here in regard to medical doctors. I thank God for them. I do not have any opposition to medical science. I say that we and the doctors are all fighting human misery, pain, sickness, and various forces that destroy and kill, so let's stick together.

> **Faith is not based on circumstances, emotions, or symptoms. It must be based simply and solely on the written Word of God.**

You are not under the law, and therefore you are perfectly free as a Christian to take the best that medical science can offer you at any time. Divine healing is not law; it is grace—a free gift God gives us through faith. Many people have come to me on occasion and said, "Well, I'm not going to the doctor." My response is, "That doesn't prove you have faith, because faith is positive and not going to the doctor is negative." I've known many people who didn't go to the doctor and died. And I have to confess that I've known many people who did go to the doctor and died, too. But faith is not represented by what you're *not* doing. Faith is positive. Faith is hearing what God says in His Word on whatever subject you need to hear and acting on it.

AN EXPERIMENT IN FAITH

I want you to follow along with me as I lead you in an experiment to help you understand the reality of the unseen Word of God in relation to healing. We must know that our faith is not based on circumstances, emotions, or symptoms. It must be based simply and solely on the written Word of God, apprehended without the natural senses. You probably know perfectly well what this type of faith is like and have experienced it. But please follow along with me in this experiment anyway.

Please answer the following question, realizing that I am not asking you to be boastful but honest. Do you know, beyond a shadow of a doubt, without the least hesitation, that all your sins have been forgiven? Do you know that God no longer counts or holds any sin against you? If you have that assurance, just say, out loud, "Yes, I do." If you answered that way, you can thank God. But don't be disconcerted or embarrassed if you didn't. If you really want to have that assurance, you can have it before you finish this chapter. However, I would advise you not to close this book until you have that assurance, even if you have to read until midnight. Who knows if you will ever get back to this matter, or even see the dawn of another day?

Here is what I want to ask of you if you said, "Yes, I do." How do you know? What evidence do you have? If you replied, "The Word of God," you are absolutely right. A dozen preachers could stand and argue with you, and you wouldn't change your opinion. A psychiatrist and a psychoanalyst and all sorts of other people could bring all their cleverest arguments against you, and you wouldn't change. Do you know why? Because, in respect to your faith in Christ and His forgiveness, you have heart faith.

You are not *trying* to believe that you are forgiven. You are not *trying* to convince yourself of the fact. You are not arguing the matter in your mind. The truth is, with heart faith, the matter is settled for you. The psalmist said, *"Forever, O LORD, Your word is settled in heaven"* (Psalm 119:89). Heart faith appropriates a

41

word that is settled in heaven. For you, the matter is decided, and that's the end of it. There is no mystery about it.

GOD SAYS IT IN HIS WORD, AND THAT SETTLES IT!

What is the point of this exercise? It is to show you that exactly the same kind of faith is needed for any transaction with the Lord—not merely for the forgiveness of sins, but also for the healing of sickness. Really, there is only one kind of faith that is acceptable to God. All you have to do in order to exercise that type of faith is to be totally committed to the fact that what God says in His Word is true.

> **Faith is needed for any transaction with the Lord—not merely for the forgiveness of sins, but also for the healing of sickness.**

Do you see the connection? You believe it is possible to know that your sins are forgiven. Because you know with certainty that your sins are forgiven, if you were seeking to lead another person into the same experience, you would encourage him not to rely on feelings. Isn't that right? You would say, "Don't base your belief on feelings. God says it, you believe it, and that settles it."

Precisely the same is true with every area of faith. You do not have faith because you *feel* that you have it. You have it because God says something and you believe it. As a result, you know what it is like to believe with your heart. But the problem with physical healing is that most people believe in it only when they see it manifested in their bodies. You would instruct a person to avoid doing that in the realm of forgiveness of sins, and it is just as wrong in the realm of physical healing. The whole basis of physical healing is exactly the same as the basis for spiritual renewal. It is nothing other than what God the Father says in His Word.

I might have a miraculous healing, and I can tell you about it, but that, by itself, doesn't give you the faintest reason to believe that God would heal you. If all I offer you is my experience, it gives you no basis for believing. The only basis is what God says in His Word. That basis of faith is the foundation we need for healing.

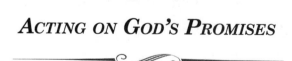

ACTING ON GOD'S PROMISES

When I lay in that hospital bed for a full year, I eventually turned to the Word of God, and I saw that I could claim healing by faith in God's written Word. I realized that, because I was a child of God, it was part of my inheritance, and I acted on that truth. I particularly acted on the promise of God in Proverbs 4:20–22:

> *My son, give attention to my words; incline your ear to my sayings. Do not let them depart from your eyes; keep them in the midst of your heart; for they are life to those who find them, and health to all their flesh.*

GOD'S "MEDICINE BOTTLE"

In the above passage, God our Father is speaking to you and me as His children. He says, "My child, if you take My words and My sayings the right way, then they are life to you and health to all your flesh." If you have health in all your flesh, you cannot have any sickness in you. That is God's basic provision.

I learned to call Proverbs 4:20–22 "God's medicine bottle." The cure is guaranteed by almighty God. The four directions are on the bottle:

1. Give attention.

2. Incline your ear to God's sayings.

3. Do not let them depart from your eyes.

4. Keep them in the midst of your heart.

Give Attention to God's Words

Here is the first direction: *"Give attention to my words"* (Proverbs 4:20). When God speaks to us, we need to give Him our undivided and respectful attention. All through the Bible, the primary key to receiving healing from God is hearing. It is what we listen to and how we listen. Are you listening with undivided attention to God's Word as you seek healing—or are you listening to something else?

It matters what we hear and how we hear. Giving attention to God's Word is not only the key to being healed, but it's also the key to receiving faith. And, of course, the two go together very closely because it is faith that enables us to receive the healing God has provided and to benefit from the medicine. Again, Romans 10:17 says, *"So then faith comes by hearing, and hearing by the word of God."*

God's Word works in us only insofar as we receive it.

In a sense, everything depends on how we approach the Word of God. Many people read the Bible but never hear God because their minds are on other things. We must put ourselves into a condition, spiritually and mentally, that enables us to hear what God is saying.

Incline Your Ear to God's Sayings

Here is the second direction: *"Incline your ear to my sayings"* (Proverbs 4:20). The verb *to incline* means to bend down, and the noun *incline* refers to something that slopes. So, inclining your ear means "bending down your ear." Physically, you cannot bend your ear without also bending your head. In inclining your ear, therefore, you are actually inclining your entire head. What does this signify? It demonstrates an attitude of humility and teachability.

God's Word works in us only insofar as we receive it. If we don't receive it, it doesn't do us any good. James wrote, *"Let every man be swift to hear, slow to speak, slow to wrath;...receive with meekness the implanted word, which is able to save your souls"* (James 1:19, 21).

God's Word can save you, heal you, and bless you in innumerable ways, but only if you receive it with meekness, or with a humble attitude—as we saw with the Syro-Phoenician woman and the Roman centurion. An essential requirement for receiving healing through the Word of God is to lay down our preconceptions and prejudices, open our ears, and listen carefully to what God says—not rejecting it because it doesn't agree with something we thought He should have said. We come to God and say, "Lord, You're the Teacher; I'm the pupil. I'm willing to let You teach me; I bow down my ear, and I listen to You."

Do Not Let God's Words Depart from Your Eyes

Here is the third direction: *"Do not let them depart from your eyes"* (Proverbs 4:21). The key thought in this direction can be summed up in the word *focus*. With natural eyesight, incorrect focus produces blurred vision, and I believe this is the problem with many people's spiritual eyesight. Unless we can focus our spiritual eyes, we will always have a blurred vision of spiritual reality.

Jesus said, *"The light of the body is the eye: therefore when thine eye is single, thy whole body also is full of light; but when thine eye is evil, thy body also is full of darkness"* (Luke 11:34 KJV). The Greek word that is translated *"single"* has various meanings. One of the main meanings is "simple" or "sincere," and I think it probably brings out the point. I would suggest that the barriers to simplicity and sincerity are sophistication and rationalization. We have to read the Bible with a single eye that affirms, "This is what God says, this is what He means, and I believe it the way it's written."

Paul wrote, *"The foolishness of God is wiser than men, and the weakness of God is stronger than men"* (1 Corinthians 1:25), and *"Let no one deceive himself. If anyone among you seems to be wise in this age, let him become a fool that he may become wise"* (1 Corinthians 3:18). Between us and God's wisdom, there is a valley—a place of humility. We have to lay aside worldly wisdom. We have to become fools in the eyes of the world so that we may really enter into God's wisdom.

Keep God's Words in the Midst of Your Heart

Here is the fourth direction: *"Keep them in the midst of your heart"* (Proverbs 4:21). The purpose of giving attention to God's words, inclining your ear to His sayings, and not letting them depart from your eyes is so that God's words and sayings will reach that vital, central area of human personality that the Bible calls the heart. When they get to the heart, they will do what is promised. But if they don't get to the heart, they won't produce the result.

In the natural world, for some medicine to be effective, it has to be released into the bloodstream, or it won't do what it's supposed to do. Spiritually, God's medicine is effective only when it's released in our hearts so that it can flow to every area of our lives. Proverbs 4:23 says, *"Keep your heart with all diligence, for out of it spring the issues of life."*

> **God's medicine is effective only when it's released in our hearts so that it can flow to every area of our lives.**

What you have in your heart will determine the course of your life. If you have the right things in your heart, your life will go right. If you have the wrong things in your heart, your life will go wrong. Keep God's Word in the midst of your heart—not just on the periphery, but in the midst. Keep it in the central place of your whole life and personality because it's going to affect the entire way that you live.

TAKE THE PRESCRIBED MEDICINE OF GOD'S WORD

Those are the four directions. If you take God's Word according to those directions, He guarantees you health. *"For they are life to those who find them, and health to all their flesh"* (Proverbs 4:22).

Once more, the directions are:

1. Give attention.

2. Incline your ear to God's sayings.

3. Do not let them depart from your eyes.

4. Keep them in the midst of your heart.

The health promised in Proverbs 4 is the basic provision of God, but it is something you must receive for yourself. I will simply leave the truth with you. It is up to you to decide whether you will take the prescribed medicine. Your healing may happen immediately. Or, it may take weeks or months. But if you take the medicine of God's Word faithfully, God has pledged Himself to make you well.

49

Chapter Four

Healing and the Cross

Exodus 15:23–26 contains a perfect picture of healing by God:

> *Now when they came to Marah, they could not drink of the waters of Marah, for they were bitter. Therefore the name of it was called Marah. And the people complained against Moses, saying, "What shall we drink?" So he cried out to the LORD, and the LORD showed him a tree. When he cast it into the waters, the waters were made sweet. There He made a statute and an ordinance for them. And there He tested them, and said, "If you diligently heed the voice of the LORD your God and do what is right in His sight, give ear to His commandments and keep all His statutes, I will put none of the diseases on you which I have brought on the Egyptians. For I am the LORD who heals you."*

This portion of Scripture is one of the great, foundational Old Testament passages on the topic of healing. I'd like to point out certain truths that arise from it.

FACETS OF THE PICTURE

God Tells Us What We Need to Know

First, the Bible doesn't tell us why the waters at Marah were bitter. Have you ever noticed that? You and I can speculate and theorize about why they were bitter, but we don't really know. Yet the Bible does tell us how the waters were made sweet.

The Bible is a very practical book. There are many situations in life that the Scriptures don't explain to us, but they do tell us what we need to know. There may be many things we don't understand and never fully will. For example, people have said to me, "Where do demons come from?" and I have replied, "You might have one idea, and I might have another. The important thing is not to know where they came from, but to know how to get rid of them. That the Bible clearly tells us."

Again, there are plenty of issues in the Bible that the natural mind might want to speculate about that are not revealed. But the things that are revealed are the things we need to know. *"The secret things belong to the LORD our God, but those things which are revealed belong to us and to our children forever, that we may do all the words of this law"* (Deuteronomy 29:29). They are revealed so that we may act on them. God may not explain to you the exact reason for every problem, suffering, need, or difficult situation that arises in your life, but He does tell you the solutions. And that is what you need to know.

Testing Is a Point of Further Revelation

Second, you will notice that the point of testing became a point of further revelation. When the Israelites arrived at the bitter waters and couldn't drink them, this was God's chosen moment to reveal Himself to them in a new aspect. The same is true for us. When

> **The Lord will use every problem as a means to show Himself greater to you than He has ever shown Himself before.**

you have come to a place of testing—a problem, a difficulty, a suffering—you can react in one of two ways. You can turn back and fail to learn the lesson. Or, you can move forward and allow the situation to be the means of a higher revelation of God for you.

God deliberately allowed the Israelites to come to the place where they were desperately thirsty. When they came to the water, it was bitter, and they could not drink it. But God brought them to that place in order to show them something more about Himself that they needed to know. Whatever happens in your life, I encourage you to be humble and sincere and to deal rightly and truly with the Lord, looking to Him in simple faith. The Lord will use every problem, difficulty, need, sickness, and hard situation as a means to show Himself greater to you than He has ever shown Himself before. Faith climbs up on obstacles. It is overcoming difficulties that gives us increased faith and spiritual character. There is no other way that character can be built.

The waters were bitter. What was the solution? What was God's revelation? Let me state it very simply. He revealed Himself as the Healer. And He revealed to Moses the basis of *all* healing. First of all, He said, *"I am the LORD who heals you."* The word in Hebrew for "who heals you" is just one word: *rapha*. Likewise, the Hebrew for doctor is *rofe*. Very legitimately, therefore, you could translate this statement as, "I am Jehovah, your Doctor." Just to illustrate this, there is a modern, very learned Hebrew medical journal in Israel called *Harofe Harivi*, which means "The Hebrew Doctor." The word *rofe* is exactly the same word and has not changed in any respect from the day of Moses, fifteen centuries before Christ, to the present era.

In every spiritual experience in which we receive provision from God, we always need to look beyond the provision to the Provider. At Marah, the provision was the tree, but the Provider was the Lord. The Lord did not allow Israel merely to receive the revelation of the tree. The revelation of the tree led to the revelation of the Lord as their Healer.

We are never intended by God to stop short at an experience, a doctrine, a revelation, or a blessing. We can thank God for every one of those things that we receive—but we cannot rest in them. Each one, in a sense, is somewhat impersonal and impermanent. Ultimately, what we need is a Person. And every true doctrine or revelation we receive will always lead us in the end to the person of God Himself. No matter how blessed the experience may be, always move on to the revelation of the Lord Himself.

The Israelites did not ask for this revelation of the Lord as their Healer; God gave it to them. What God said then about being "Jehovah, your Doctor" is every bit as true today for you and me. God has not changed. In Malachi 3:6, right at the close of the Old Testament, He says, *"For I am the Lord* [Jehovah], *I do not change."* Hebrews 13:8, in the New Testament, says, *"Jesus Christ is the same yesterday, today, and forever."* The same Jehovah who was His people's Doctor then is His people's Doctor today. This is a fact. It is His will, irrespective of our wills.

Just as truly as the Lord is your Savior, He is your Doctor. We must understand this truth: He is Doctor Jehovah.

THE HEALING TREE

The incident at Marah occurred shortly after the Israelites had been miraculously liberated from slavery in Egypt and had passed through the waters of the Red Sea as though on dry land. Then, the Egyptians were swept away when God brought back the waters over them, putting an end to the entire contingent of the enemy that was pursuing His people.

This was a tremendous triumph. The Israelites had experienced a glorious deliverance. They were exultant; they felt everything was under God's control. Then, they were led by God through Moses into the wilderness of Shur, where they went for three days without finding water. Of course, they had an emergency supply of water in their water skins, but that must have been running low; the children and the cattle were beginning to become thirsty; they were all weary from the hot and dusty journey. And then, in the distance, they saw the gleam of water in a pool. I'm sure some of them started to run to get there to quench their thirst. But, oh, what a bitter disappointment when they stooped down to drink!

The Israelites began to complain and murmur against Moses. Think of the noise of all those people complaining and murmuring at once! Yet, in the midst of the murmuring, one man—Moses—had the sense to pray. And he got the answer. Let me just say that when faced with a difficulty, you can either murmur or pray. If you murmur, that is your choice, but it won't help the situation. If you pray, the Lord will show you the answer.

The Key That Unlocks the Power

While the Israelites chose to complain about the bitter waters they encountered at Marah, Moses prayed, and the answer the Lord showed him was a tree. When he cast it into the bitter waters, the waters were made sweet. This is the healing tree.

When you want God's miracle-working power to operate, you sometimes have to perform a very simple act.

The Scriptures do not say that the tree healed the waters. In fact, I don't believe that was the case. I believe the supernatural power of God did the healing. But Moses' act of faith in casting in the tree unlocked this supernatural power. This is a great principle in regard to God. When you want His miracle-working power to operate, you sometimes have to perform a very simple act. The act, in itself, does not generate the power—but it is the key that unlocks the power.

Simple Acts of Faith

The prophet Elisha grasped this principle. He faced a situation similar to what the Israelites had faced at Marah. The waters in Jericho were bad, and they didn't produce a fruitful soil. When the inhabitants asked him to intervene, Elisha took a bowl of salt and cast the salt into the source of the water, and the waters became sweet. (See 2 Kings 2:19–22.) It wasn't the salt that made the waters sweet—it was God's miraculous power.

Likewise, when there were poisonous gourds in a pot of stew, Elisha took some flour and put it into the pot, and the stew was made healthy. (See 2 Kings 4:38–41.) It wasn't the flour that made the stew healthy—it was God's miraculous power.

When Elisha wanted to raise a boy from the dead, he ordered that his staff be put on the child's face. (See 2 Kings 4:8–37.) It wasn't the staff that held back the power of death. But it was God's miraculous power!

Let's look at two ordinances for healing found in the New Testament that require simple acts of faith. The first is found in Mark 16:17–18: *"These signs will follow those who believe: In My name...they will lay hands on the sick, and they will recover."* The Scriptures don't say that our hands will heal the sick. They say that when we lay our hands on the sick, they will get better.

When I was in the British army and was released from the hospital in Egypt, I was transferred to the Sudan, and I ended up in an area called the Red Sea Hills. I was the only corporal in a small British military hospital with about forty beds. The only regular patients we had were Italian prisoners of war who had surrendered in Ethiopia or North Africa. One of my responsibilities was to oversee the native Sudanese labor force that was responsible for cleaning the hospital.

That region of the Sudan was 100 percent Muslim. The British government, which ruled over the area at that time, would not permit any Christian missionaries access because they did not want to infuriate the Muslims. But the British army sent one poor, humble British corporal right into the very center of that area. As I was getting ready to be transferred, God gave me a supernatural burden of prayer for the people of Sudan. A prayer burden is something you cannot understand if you have not experienced it. I could not sleep at night because I felt compelled to pray for those people. There was nothing in the natural to connect us. In many ways, the people were primitive and very unsympathetic. But God gave me that tremendous burden of prayer before placing me in the Sudan in charge of the native laborers at the hospital.

My liaison with this labor force was a Muslim man named Ali. I don't think he had ever been to school, but he was very smart, and he was a first-rate soccer player. Yet he was also a very bad man. He was a brawler and a drunkard—which no Muslim should be because Muslims are not allowed to consume strong drink. He also took a percentage from the pay of everyone whom he employed, cheating them of their wages.

Yet Ali was my only point of contact with the Sudanese, and I felt a deep desire to communicate to him what I knew about Jesus Christ. At this time, I was a fairly new Christian, having gotten saved just before being shipped to Africa with the army, and I had no training from a church or Bible school. I was in the Red Sea Hills for eight months, but for the first four months, I could not find any way to connect with Ali in a personal way in order to share Jesus with him.

Ali spoke English, which he had picked up from the British military personnel, but it was essentially "soldiers' English." Soldiers' English was not the most refined or elegant dialect, but it was pretty vivid, and he understood it. He also had a fantastic memory, which is often the case with people who have never learned to read or write. For instance, one of the things we had to do was to get the bugs out of people's blankets. This process was known as *disinfestation.*

The average British soldier had to hear that word half a dozen times before he got it right. Ali heard it once and never got it wrong from that point on. His memory by ear was amazingly acute.

One day, Ali said something to me about Satan. When I discovered he believed in Satan, I immediately let him know that I believed in Satan, too. Ironically, that was our point of contact. I told him all the trouble the devil made for me, and he told me the trouble the devil made for him. So, we had finally made a personal connection.

Ali used to come and meet me in my area about nine o'clock every morning. One morning, he was nearly an hour late. When he came in, he was apologetic and said, "I'm sorry, but I had to go to the hospital to have my foot treated." I asked, "What's the matter with your foot?" and he said, "It's got a sore on it. I've been having it treated for two months, but it won't heal."

At that moment, Mark 16:17–18 came to me: *"And these signs shall follow them that believe; in my name shall they...lay hands on the sick, and they shall recover"* (KJV). Even though I felt as cold as ice because of my nervousness, I asked him, "Would you like me to pray for you?" He said yes. He obviously felt he couldn't lose anything by it. "All right," I said, "I will pray for you. But I'll tell you one thing: I am praying in the name of Jesus." He said, "All right."

As far as I can remember, I had never before seen anybody lay hands on the sick and pray for them. I didn't know how to do it; I had no pattern. So, I stood at a safe distance, stretched out my hands, put them somewhere on his body, and said a very short prayer. If you had asked me at the time how much faith I had, I would have said, "Zero." Yet, a week later, he came in, and his face was shining. He asked, "Shall I show you my foot?" I said yes, and I saw that it was completely healed. God had done it.

Let me give you an addendum to this story. After Ali was healed, He listened to me, so I thought I would try to tell him about Jesus. He was receptive, so I began reading him a short passage from the New Testament every morning. I read the King James Version, but as I read, I would change the words into soldiers' English—which was quite an undertaking!

> *I stretched out my hands, put them somewhere on his body, and said a very short prayer. A week later, his foot was completely healed. God had done it.*

This went on for a while. Then, one night, when I went back to my room to go to sleep, I threw myself on my bed in the dark—and felt the sharpest, most intense pain I had ever experienced in my life. I jumped off the bed, switched on the light, and realized I had been stung by a hornet. Let me tell you: Sudanese hornets are in a class by themselves! I was in great pain and full of fear, but the verse came to me, *"Behold, I give unto you power to tread on serpents and scorpions, and over all the power of the enemy: and nothing shall by any means hurt you"* (Luke 10:19 KJV).

I thought, *If it says serpents and scorpions, it must apply to hornets, too.* For ten minutes, I walked up and down, limping across the floor of that room with my arms in the air, praising God and thanking Him that it couldn't hurt me. At the end of ten minutes, the pain had left. The hole was still visible in my ankle, but there was not the faintest trace of swelling.

The next day, I met Ali in the my area, as usual, and I said, "You know, something happened to me last night." He asked, "What?" and I said, "A hornet stung me." He said, "A hornet stung you?" I said, "Yes, would you like to see where?" and pulled my sock down and showed him the hole in my ankle. "And it didn't swell?" he asked. When I said no, he said, "I can't understand that." He took me to the door, pointed to a man who happened to be hobbling across the compound of the hospital at that time with one knee bent, and said, "You see that man? You know why his knee is bent? He was stung by a hornet, and it never straightened out." After that, Ali was doubly willing to listen to what I had to say!

With this testimony in mind, let's now return to our original point about the ordinance of laying hands on the sick for healing—such as I did in laying hands on Ali for his foot to be healed. Laying on hands is a simple act in obedience to God the Father that unlocks His miracle-working power. In addition, my own healing from the hornet's sting was a demonstration of what happens when we believe and act on God's Word.

Another ordinance is described in James 5:14–15:

Is anyone sick among you sick? Let him call for the elders of the church, and let them pray over him, anointing him with oil in the name of the Lord. And the prayer of faith will save the sick, and the Lord will raise him up.

Applying the oil does not heal the person, and the oil itself doesn't heal. It is the miraculous power of God that heals. But applying the oil is the simple act that unlocks the miracle-working power of God. The oil is a type of the Holy Spirit. It is an outward act by which we testify to our faith that the same Spirit who raised up Jesus from the dead can quicken and heal the sick body of a child of God.

One of the great revelations in the Word of God, then, is that a simple act of faith is often required to unlock God's miracle-working power. The acts we have just looked at were very simple. Sometimes, the acts that God asks us to perform are almost childish—even silly to the natural mind. In John 9, we read about an occasion when Jesus put clay on a blind man's eyes and said, *"Go, wash in the pool of Siloam"* (verse 7). Neither the clay nor the pool of Siloam changed that man's eyes. It was the miracle-working power of God that healed him. But these two simple acts were required to unlock God's miracle-working power: first, the application of clay by Jesus; second, the washing in the pool by the man.

The next time you have a problem that you can't resolve, remember that a simple act of faith can release the miracle-working power of God. Faith without works is dead. (See James 2:20, 26.) If you don't do anything, you don't have faith. Many times, people will not move out in faith because they think, *I might look like a fool.* Nothing inhibits our faith more than the fear of looking foolish, isn't that true? But Moses was willing to look like a fool at the bitter waters of Marah. He took that piece of wood and threw it into the water with a splash. Everybody could see it, and everybody could hear it. Yet the result was that everybody could drink the water.

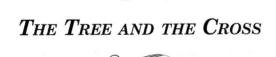

THE TREE AND THE CROSS

What I share next is the ultimate expression of the truth we have been discussing, *"I am the LORD who heals you"* (Exodus 15:26). It is the revelation of

Jesus as the Healer. Everything you need to know is based on this revelation, for it explains the ultimate means of healing.

This Old Testament event at Marah foreshadowed the cross of Jesus and the healing we receive through it. Moses was told to cast a tree into the water to take away its bitterness. The word *tree* in the Hebrew language is sometimes hard to specify. I encountered a similar linguistic difficulty when I went to East Africa. The people who spoke Swahili used the same word for tree, whether it was a tree that was growing or a tree that had been cut down. Either way, it was just a "tree."

Many people don't understand why the cross is referred to as a tree in many Bible translations, yet, in Hebrew, as in Swahili, the word for tree is used whether it is alive and growing or cut down. Moses was told to cut down a tree and cast it into the waters—and this tree is a type of the cross of Jesus Christ.

> **The very heart of the gospel message is that the cross is the whole basis of healing.**

The very heart of the gospel message is that the cross is the whole basis of healing. Everything in the gospel centers on the cross. The cross is the meeting place of every aspect of human need with God's provision. There is no other meeting place. No matter what your need may be, it is solved at Calvary.

A friend of mine, who was an earnest Christian, worked in the office of the city hall in London. Like millions of people, he went to work every morning and back home every evening carrying a briefcase. I suppose all that is inside some office workers' briefcases are sandwiches for lunch. But if you worked in the city of London, you just had to carry a briefcase. You hadn't "arrived" until you did.

This particular friend carried a very good briefcase, but he had printed something on it in big, black, capital letters that made his briefcase different from the others: GOD WAITS TO MEET YOU AT CALVARY. That phrase has always gripped my imagination. It is so true. God waits to meet you at Calvary. There is only one place where you will meet God, and it is at the cross. On the cross, everything that stood between you and God was dealt with once and for all. That is God's appointed meeting place.

I heard another story that captured my imagination as well. In the city of Glasgow, Scotland, there is a well-known central meeting place of various main streets called "The Cross." One day, a little girl who lived in Glasgow strayed from her home. Soon she didn't know where she was, and she started to cry. She sat down on the edge of a curb and began to wipe the tears from her eyes with grimy fingers. Her face got grimier and grimier. After a while, a big, kindly policeman came along. He saw this little girl crying and asked her what was the matter. She said, "Please, I'm lost. I don't know the way home." He said to her, "Come with me to the police station, and we'll start to make inquiries." The policeman took her by the hand and began to lead her. It so happened that the way to the police station led through this big central meeting area. When the policeman got to "The Cross," he felt the little girl's hand tugging at his, so he looked down at her and asked, "What's the matter?" She said, "Please, sir, it's all right now. I know the way home from here."

And that is true for us as well. The cross is the sinner's way home. When you have gotten to the cross, you can find your way home. It is the meeting place between God and man.

OUR SOURCE OF HEALING

On the cross, Jesus bore in His own body every burden that could come onto a fallen, sin-cursed race. First Peter 2:24 says, "[He] *Himself bore our sins in His own body on the tree, that we, having died to sins, might live for righteousness; by whose stripes you were healed."* Again, the Greek verb for *"healed"* in this verse is the word that specifically denotes physical healing. There is no question that it means physical healing. By the atoning, substitutionary sacrifice of Jesus Christ on the cross, complete physical healing was provided for every believer.

> **By the atoning, substitutionary sacrifice of Jesus Christ on the cross, complete physical healing was provided for every believer.**

As we have been discussing, Jesus did not bear only our sins on the cross, but also our sicknesses. Matthew 8:16–17 says, *"He...healed all who were sick, that it might be fulfilled which was spoken by Isaiah the prophet, saying: 'He Himself took our infirmities and bore our sicknesses.'"* You have the legal right to perfect healing because every sickness, every infirmity, every pain that sin brought upon the human race was laid upon the body of Jesus as He hung on the cross. He was the sinner's substitute. Everything that was due to the sinner was laid upon Him.

That is the only basis by which God can forgive your sins—that Jesus bore your sins and paid your penalty. Likewise, that is the only final basis for divine healing—the fact that Jesus took your infirmities and bore your sicknesses, and that by His stripes you were healed. This is the revelation of the Bible, the Word of God, and it never varies. There isn't any passage in the Scriptures that is not in perfect line with it.

Chapter Five

Choosing Jesus as Your Physician

We have seen that the only basis for your receiving divine healing is the fact that Jesus took your infirmities and bore your sicknesses on the cross, and that by His stripes you were healed. This is the unchanging revelation of the Bible, the Word of God. You have heard that revelation, and now you have an opportunity to respond in faith. *"So then faith comes by hearing, and hearing by the word of God"* (Romans 10:17).

THE POINT OF DECISION

After you hear God's Word, you come to a moment of decision. You must decide if you are going to respond. No one else can make this decision for you in relation to physical healing: Are you going to accept Jesus Christ as your Physician? That is who He is. We need to bring this down to a very practical level. If you make the decision, are you going to follow it up with a commitment?

When you go to the doctor, and he tells you to take pills, you have to take them if you want the cure. When he tells you that you need surgery, you must submit to the procedure if you want to correct the problem. Otherwise, your decision to go to that doctor is fruitless. It is exactly the same with the Lord. There is no decision in relation to Him that does not involve a commitment. Will you commit your case to Him without reservation? Nothing that follows depends on what you see or feel. It depends on your hearing, believing, and acting on the Word—making a decision and following it by commitment.

If, after reading the truths I have shared, you are merely hoping that the Lord will heal you of the affliction you are facing, stop the experiment right now. If you are just trying it out, seeing if it works, that's not faith. Faith is not an experiment. It is a commitment.

But if, after what you have read, you have truly heard the Word of God and have made a decision, then move forward in faith. Make this declaration: "I am going to trust the Son of God to be my personal Physician. I am going to commit myself and my case to Him without reservation. I am going to renounce anything that might come between the Lord and me—any kind of sin, carnality, worldliness, indifference, and lukewarmness. And I am going to take much more time with His precious Word, because that is where the lifeline is." If you really want to have your need ministered to, then, and only then, move forward in faith.

This may seem like a strange kind of appeal, because it might appear as if I am almost trying to hold you back. But I hope you understand the seriousness of this decision. In Africa, if you want to make an appeal for salvation, you have to take the same approach. It is possible to preach to an African congregation in certain places and have 90 percent of the people come forward for salvation. You actually have to make it more difficult for people to respond so that they truly understand what they are committing to. The great problem that I had in Africa was trying to stop the same people from coming forward every week for salvation. You may laugh at their response, but that is exactly what happens with many people in regard to healing. Why? Because people do not commit! They respond only as an experiment, saying, "Well, I'll go forward and see if this preacher can do anything for me," or "This brother and that brother prayed for me already. Now, see if you can do it." Frankly, I object to being the next name on someone's list.

"Do You Want My Services?"

Let me ask you these questions: Do you think the Lord is a competent Doctor? Do you really believe He knows His job? In the natural realm, a doctor never attends a patient professionally unless he is invited to—except in an emergency. Under normal circumstances, you have to choose your doctor. Your family physician is not your doctor because he wanted to be but because you chose him. It is exactly the same with the Lord. He is potentially your Doctor, but you have to actually make Him your Doctor by choice. You make Him your Doctor when you believe that He is trustworthy to attend to your needs.

Again, we see that there are certain basic principles of faith that apply just as much in the physical realm of healing as they do in forgiveness of sin. Most of us are familiar with the ministry of Billy Graham. You probably either watched one of his crusades on television or were present at one. I have done both, myself. Basically, what Billy Graham did for about forty-five minutes was to preach what the Scriptures teach about forgiveness of sin and salvation. Then, having preached, he invited the people to make a decision. The word *decision* was a key word in his vocabulary.

Some segments of the church may object slightly to this method, but, on the whole, when a Billy Graham crusade reported that there were 3000 "decisions" for Christ, we understood what they were talking about. It meant that 3000 people came to the place where they made a decision to accept Jesus as Savior. Billy Graham never allowed those who made that decision to remain passive in their seats. He always called them out and demanded that they make a personal commitment. That is faith. It is hearing the Word, making a decision, and following it up with a commitment.

Precisely the same is true with physical healing. You hear the Word, and then you make a decision. What is your decision? Have you decided, "I want the Lord to be my Doctor"? When you have done that, you make a commitment—you commit your case to Him. It is exactly parallel. There is no difference. What works in the spiritual realm works every bit as well in the physical realm. Jesus says, "I am the Lord, your Doctor. Do you want My services?"

Have you told Him that you want Him to be your Doctor? Have you made that decision?

CHOOSING MEANS HEART FAITH, NOT EMOTION

Once more, to illustrate all this from the realm of forgiveness of sins, you would not expect a person to receive salvation apart from the Savior, would you?

Some people would like to have their sins forgiven, because sin is a great burden, but they don't want the Savior. However, we don't teach them that they can have salvation without the Savior. Neither can you have healing without the Healer. It is a personal commitment to Jesus as Healer. It is a decision, not an emotion. You don't have to get very emotional when you pick up the phone and call your doctor. Sometimes people do, but, on the whole, it is in the realm of decision. Emotion is not faith, but decision is.

As we discussed earlier, we know very well what heart faith is if we put it in the context of salvation. Heart faith for salvation is a decision, independent of the emotions. You may feel tremendous emotion, or you may feel none. I have seen some people receive the most wonderful experience of conversion without any evidence of emotion. They neither trembled nor shook nor sobbed.

I know of a man who sponsored and was the chairman for the Billy Graham crusade in Chicago some years back. And I happen to know the man who led him to the Lord. He was a friend of mine who was a member of a Baptist church. At the time my friend led him to Christ, this man was the president of a bank. One day, after the morning service in the Baptist church, this bank president came into the inquiry room of the office to be counseled. And my friend gave him the plan of salvation, as a good Baptist would— Romans 3:23, Romans 6:23, and so on and so forth. All went well. My friend said that the other man took the whole thing exactly as if he were in his bank, signing a contract. There was no emotion, so that my friend couldn't determine whether it was real or not. And yet that bank president became one of the outstanding Christians of his community. He made a decision based on the Word, not emotion.

Sometimes, we need to get our emotions out of the way. The majority of people in some movements confuse emotionalism with faith, and with the moving of the Holy Spirit. Years ago, some people from New Zealand said to me, "We've never met a preacher who makes a less emotional appeal than you do." Well, emotion is not the issue. You can get people sobbing and weeping. You can jump up and down on the platform and get all excited. Yet, in my opinion, you may just distract people's attention from the real issue. Emotion is not the goal. The heart is not moved primarily by emotion. It is moved by decision. Those two responses are very different.

Similarly, repentance is a decision. Many people get very emotional about their sins but never repent. We see them at the altar of the church every Sunday doing a little weeping, crying on somebody's shoulder. Then, they go on living in the same wrong way and come back to have a little sob the next week. They display emotion, but not true repentance. They probably don't really understand what is needed. They need to make the decision to turn from their sins and follow God.

Exactly the same step is needed in the realm of healing. Who is going to be your doctor? Again, your human physician will not force his services upon you. Neither will your Divine Physician. You have to make the decision to choose Him.

A CONTINUAL DECISION TO WALK IN HEALING

There is another aspect to the verse *"I am the LORD who heals you"* (Exodus 15:26) that relates to your decision to make the Lord your Physician. In actual fact, the above statement is in the continuous present tense: "I am the Lord who is healing you." If you are living in contact with the Lord, He is healing you all the time. It is a continual process.

It is just like 1 John 1:7: *"If we walk in the light as He is in the light, we have fellowship with one another, and the blood of Jesus Christ His Son cleanses us* [continually] *from all sin."* If you are in a right relationship with God and man, you are being cleansed all the time by the blood of Jesus. Likewise, if you are in this relationship with God, He is healing you all the time.

> **If you are in this relationship with God, He is healing you all the time.**

77

You may think this is a silly thought, but you don't have to wait to get sick to thank God for healing you—because He is healing you all the time. Every morning, when you look in the mirror, you can say, "Thank You, Jesus, that You took my infirmities and bore my sicknesses. That's why I'm healthy." You will feel much better after doing that. That acknowledgment and gratitude for healing is your decision. And it can be your attitude in relationship to God.

THE POWER OF COVENANT

Furthermore, one of the great revelations that comes as we study the statement "I am the Lord who is healing you" is the principle of covenant. On the grounds of this promise, God made a covenant with Israel. It is very interesting that God has decided to operate on the basis of covenants. Normally, everything that God does in relationship to man is done on the basis of a covenant.

I discovered this truth when I first began to read the Bible in Hebrew and made up my mind (I'm sure it was the Holy Spirit who inspired me) that I was going to follow certain themes through the Bible. Here is what I decided to do: I would take three colored pencils—a blue pencil, a green pencil, and a red pencil.

The blue was for marking passages related to covenant, the green was for passages related to sacrifice, and the red was for passages related to the shedding of blood. I had no idea in advance that it would turn out this way, but everywhere I had the blue, I also had the green and the red. The reason? You cannot have a covenant without a sacrifice, and you cannot have a sacrifice without the shedding of blood.

This reality is summed up in Psalm 50:5, where the Lord says, *"Gather My saints together to Me, those who have made a covenant with Me by sacrifice."* In all ages, God's people have been those who have made a covenant with Him on the basis of sacrifice. There is no way to enter into a relationship of acceptance with God other than on the basis of a covenant.

THE CHILDREN'S BREAD

We find an interesting outworking of the principle of covenant in Matthew 15. When Jesus was going through the length and breadth of Israel, the Scriptures tell us that He healed everyone who came to Him.

Then great multitudes came to Him, having with them the lame, blind, mute, maimed, and many others; and they laid them down at

79

Jesus' feet, and He healed them. So the multitude marveled when they saw the mute speaking, the maimed made whole, the lame walking, and the blind seeing; and they glorified the God of Israel. (Matthew 15:30–31)

Every Israelite who came to Jesus received healing. He never once refused, and He never questioned. Why? Because fifteen centuries earlier, God had committed Himself in a covenant.

Recall that when the Syro-Phoenician woman, a Gentile, cried out to the Lord to heal her daughter, He did not immediately respond. (See Matthew 15:22–23.) When she tried to persuade Him, He said, *"It is not good to take the children's bread and throw it to the little dogs"* (verse 26). Some people don't like to believe that Jesus told that woman she was a dog, but He did. And she understood perfectly well what He meant. Even so, she said, *"Yes, Lord, yet even the little dogs eat the crumbs which fall from their masters' table"* (verse 27). That answer got her the jackpot, you might say. *"Then Jesus answered and said to her, 'O woman, great is your faith! Let it be to you as you desire'"* (verse 28). I would be happy to hear that from the Lord, wouldn't you?

Do you really understand, however, why Jesus called her a "dog"? It was because, under the law, she wasn't in a covenantal relationship with God. She was outside the covenant; she was considered unclean. A dog is an unclean animal. And every person who is outside a covenantal relationship with God is unclean. The only basis for being acceptable before God was this covenantal relationship, yet even a woman outside the covenant received what she asked for because of her great faith.

The New Testament tells us of the new covenant with God the Father that anyone—Jew or Gentile—can receive through the blood of the Lord Jesus Christ. The only way to be acceptable to God is to enter into a covenantal relationship with Him by receiving Christ as Savior. There is no other way. God may heal someone outside this covenant, but our salvation depends on it.

> **"Give us this day our daily bread"** *can refer to healing or health— healing is the children's bread.*

We need to remember another very important fact from this story of the Syro-Phoenician woman, which we noted earlier: If you are a child of God, healing is your bread. Jesus said, *"I am the bread of life"* (John 6:35, 48). You may have grown up in a home where there weren't many luxuries. Yet your parents probably never denied you bread. Bread was part of your basic right in the family. The same is true with God. Your heavenly Father will never deny you bread. (See Matthew 7:9.)

Jesus said that we are to pray, every day, *"Give us this day our daily bread"* (Matthew 6:11). This *"bread"* can refer to our sustenance, our need for God's Word, and even to healing or health—because healing is the children's bread.

If the "crumbs" could get the demon out of that woman's daughter, what will the crumbs do for you? And you don't have to live on the crumbs—if you are a child of God, you are entitled to the loaf! Will you allow Him to give it to you? Will you let Him be your Physician?

TAKE TIME TO PRAY

To close this chapter, let's take some time to pray. Become reverent and quiet and alone with God. Don't allow yourself to be distracted by what is around you. Remember, faith does not see with natural eyes. If you are looking with natural eyes, it is not faith.

Right now, you may be coming to the Lord with a definite personal need. It may be spiritual, or it may be physical. You may not have real inward peace. You may need the assurance that your sins are forgiven and that you have a true covenantal relationship with God. Or, you may need physical deliverance through healing. Tell the Lord you want to bring your case to Him right now without reservation. Express your willingness by making that confession to Him and preparing your heart for the commitment prayer below. This is an important decision, and I want you to go through with it.

Now, I want you to follow me in a definite, simple prayer. First, I want you to make a deliberate, personal confession of faith and commitment to Jesus Christ. If you are already saved, it won't do the least bit of harm to say it again. Would you read these words, saying them directly to Jesus?

Lord Jesus Christ, I believe that You are the Son of God. You died on the cross for my sins. You bore my sicknesses. You took my infirmities. You shed Your blood for me. You rose again from the dead. I come to You now by simple faith, and I claim Your promise that *"the one who comes to Me I will by no means cast out."* Lord, I have come to You, and I believe You have received me. I commit myself to You now without reservation—spirit, soul, and body. I put myself into Your hands as my Physician. Lord Jesus, be my Doctor—I want Your services. Save me, heal me, and make me whole, for Your glory. In Jesus' name, amen.

By faith, thank Him for receiving your confession and commitment to Him.

Chapter Six

The Healing Message of Jesus: The Gospel of the Kingdom

In Jesus' earthly ministry of healing, there were two distinct aspects—the *message* He spoke and the *methods* He used. In this chapter, we will focus on His message as we continue to build on the biblical foundations for healing.

Let us begin by noting what is written about Jesus' disciples in the last verse of Mark's gospel. The background is that Jesus had just ascended to heaven, after giving them these instructions:

Go into all the world and preach the gospel to every creature....And these signs will follow those who believe: In My name they will cast out demons; they will speak with new tongues; they will take up serpents; and if they drink anything deadly, it will by no means hurt them; they will lay hands on the sick, and they will recover. (Mark 16:15, 17–18)

Then, we read:

And they went out and preached everywhere, the Lord working with them and confirming the word through the accompanying signs.

(Mark 16:20)

I want to point out to you that it is the *word* that the Lord confirms with miracles. If you want the right miracles, logic would indicate that you must have the right word. You cannot expect God to confirm a word that isn't the word He is prepared to confirm!

Likewise, Acts 14:3 speaks about the ministry of Paul and Barnabas in Iconium:

They stayed there a long time, speaking boldly in the Lord, who was bearing witness to the word of His grace, granting signs and wonders to be done by their hands.

Notice again that the signs and wonders came because the Lord was bearing witness to *"the word of His grace."* It was this word that He attested by the miracles. Once more, the conclusion is obvious: If you get the wrong word, you cannot expect the attesting miracles.

GETTING THE GOSPEL MESSAGE RIGHT

For many centuries, much of the church really has not presented the message of the gospel as it was presented in the New Testament. I would say that it has been truncated. Part of it has been cut off, and now the message that we are accustomed to calling "the gospel" is, in actual fact, only a portion of the real gospel. In a certain sense, the most important part has been left out.

> **The word gospel means "good news," and that includes healing.**

Bear in mind that the word *gospel* means "good news." I frequently tell people that if you ever hear anything that is not good news, realize that it is not the gospel. There is much so-called gospel preaching that contains precious little good news.

I knew a dear brother who was a deacon in a very famous fundamentalist church in Chicago. He was a well-educated man—a doctor of theology, and so on—and a committed Christian. His wife developed a disease of the kidneys. They went to a Jewish specialist who happened to be an agnostic or atheist, and he was the one who diagnosed the disease. He told them, "There is no cure." So, she went to the bookshop of their church, which was a very famous bookshop, to look for a book on healing. Afterward, she told me, "I found fourteen books on how to suffer but not one on how to be healed."

In desperation, this couple did something that fundamentalists would normally never do. They went

THE HEALING MESSAGE OF JESUS: THE GOSPEL OF THE KINGDOM

to a high Episcopal church, where the rector anointed the wife with oil in the name of the Lord, and she was healed. When she went back to the doctor, he said, "This is a miracle!" Well, that's good news. So, bear in mind, we are talking about the good news of the gospel, and that includes healing.

THE KINGDOM, OR GOVERNMENT, OF GOD

The standard phrase used in the New Testament is *"the gospel of the kingdom,"* or, "the good news of the kingdom." (See, for example, Matthew 4:23.) It is unscriptural to leave out the words "the kingdom" when presenting the gospel. The gospel is not just some vague piece of good news. It is not, as it is usually represented, simply the fact that you can repent and have your sins forgiven and receive eternal life. I thank God that is true, but it is not the complete story. It is, as it were, a stepping-stone to God's ultimate purpose. What a shame it would be if you started to cross a stream on stepping-stones but stopped when you got to the middle and never moved any farther. How tragic to always be on the same stepping-stone, never reaching the other shore.

> **The solution to human problems is for man to come back under God's government.**

Sadly, that is the condition, I would say, of most of the church today.

What, then, is the essence of the good news of the kingdom? According to my understanding, it is this: that God the Father is willing to take over the governance of the human race. Keep in mind that in the Bible, "kingdom" is the normal form of government. Democracy, as we know it, was unknown. When the Bible speaks about a kingdom, it is talking about a form of government.

If you analyze human history, you see that all of man's problems started when he rejected the government of God. The only solution to human problems that will ultimately work is for man to come back under God's government. The good news is that God is willing to take man back under His governance.

There is such an attitude of rebellion and independence in the world today that most people don't like the word *government*. They don't see it as good news. But you cannot receive the gospel in the New Testament sense unless you are prepared to accept and submit to the righteous governance of God in your life.

FIVE PHASES OF THE GOSPEL OF THE KINGDOM

There are five phases of the gospel of the kingdom, or the good news of the government of God. As it happens, all five phases begin with the letters *pr*: *prediction, proclamation, proof, prayer,* and *priority.* Recognizing these phases gives us a foundation for understanding the full gospel message.

The Prediction of the Kingdom

One of the most widely accepted *predictions* of the coming of Jesus as Messiah is the proclamation found in Isaiah 9:

> *For unto us a Child is born, unto us a Son is given.* (verse 6)

That prediction of a *"Child,"* or *"Son,"* was fulfilled in the birth of Jesus.

> *And the government will be upon His shoulder. And His name will be called Wonderful, Counselor, Mighty God, Everlasting Father, Prince of Peace.* (verse 6)

The first statement about this child is that *"the government will be upon His shoulder."* All those names that follow are related to Jesus' governance. They are aspects of His character and nature that qualify Him to govern. The next verse says,

> *Of the increase of His government and peace there will be no end.* (verse 7)

Notice that the word *government* is doubly stressed in this passage, and that peace follows government. I believe that true peace is possible only under the government of Jesus Christ. Those who are not governed by Jesus Christ do not know peace—whether they are individuals, families, nations, or all humanity. If you try to achieve peace without the government of Jesus, you are going to be frustrated. The increase of His government, of His righteous rule and peace, will have no end.

Next, the passage says,

Upon the throne of David and over His kingdom.... (verse 7)

What kind of a government was the Messiah going to have? A kingdom. That is very clear.

The Proclamation of the Kingdom

To see the New Testament outworking of the above prophecy, we will turn to Matthew's gospel. Matthew is the first of the books in the New Testament, and it is the gospel of the King—it frequently mentions the King and the kingdom.

Let us look at what we might call the *proclamation* of the kingdom, given by John the Baptist, the man who was sent ahead of Jesus to prepare the way for Him.

In those days John the Baptist came preaching [proclaiming] *in the wilderness of Judea, and*

*saying, "Repent, for the kingdom of heaven is at
hand!"* (Matthew 3:1–2)

I prefer to translate the word *preaching* as *proclaiming* in the above passage because the verb in the original Greek is directly related to the noun for a herald. What does a herald do? He proclaims.

Why is the kingdom introduced with the requirement to repent? Because we are all, by nature, rebels against God—every one of us.

*All we like sheep have gone astray; we have
turned, every one, to his own way* [rebelled];
and the LORD has laid on [Jesus] *the iniquity*
[rebellion] *of us all.* (Isaiah 53:6)

We have all turned to our own ways. There are no exceptions. We have not all committed murder or adultery or gotten drunk, but there is not one of us who hasn't been guilty of rebellion in going his own way. And the Bible says very clearly that our ways are not God's ways. (See, for example, Isaiah 55:7–9.)

Consequently, there is no way back under the government of God except by repentance. And, again, repentance is not emotion. It is a decision. It means you come to your senses, you see the truth about yourself, you realize what kind of a person you really are—what a mess you're in. In the parable of the prodigal son, the prodigal went away from his father and his home and got into an awful mess—until he finally came to himself. (See Luke 15:11–24.) The same is necessary for us. We have to come to ourselves. We have to see the real truth about ourselves. We are rebels by nature—rebels by choice and rebels by deed. There is no way into the kingdom of God for anybody who bypasses repentance.

Repentance says, "Lord, I've been going my own way. I've been doing my own thing. I've been believing what I wanted to believe. I've been setting my own standards. Maybe I've been religious, but I have been pleasing only myself. I've come to the end of that. Forgive me. Here I am, Lord. Tell me what to do, and I will do it."

In the years I spent counseling Christians, I came to the conclusion that at least 50 percent of all the problems Christians have are caused by a failure to repent. If these Christians had really practiced repentance, most of their problems would have ceased to exist. A person who has repented never argues with God. He simply says, "Here I am, God. I'm sorry. There's nothing I can do to make amends, but, from now on, whatever You say, I'll do." That's repentance.

John the Baptist fulfilled his course, and he was put in prison as Jesus was beginning His public ministry. I believe that Jesus paid John the greatest compliment He could ever pay anybody. He started His ministry with exactly the same word that John had. I can't think of anything that would honor me more than if the Lord would echo my preaching. In Matthew 4:17, we read,

> *From that time Jesus began to preach* [proclaim] *and to say, "Repent, for the kingdom of heaven is at hand."*

That is *the* message. No one has any right to truncate it or pervert it.

The Proof of the Kingdom

Next, we come to the *proof* of the kingdom. Let's continue reading in Matthew 4:

> *And Jesus went about all Galilee, teaching in their synagogues, preaching the gospel of the kingdom* [proclaiming the good news of the kingdom], *and healing all kinds of sickness and all kinds of disease among the people. Then His fame went throughout all Syria; and they brought to Him all sick people who were afflicted with various diseases and torments, and those who were demon-possessed, epileptics, and paralytics; and He healed them.*
> (Matthew 4:23–24)

In the terminology of the day, verse 24 lists every kind of affliction and infirmity—mental, emotional, and physical—that anybody could experience. And it says that Jesus healed all kinds of sickness and all kinds of infirmity. Why? Because that was the proof that the kingdom had come.

Wherever the kingdom of God is truly established, sin and sickness are banished.

This is the crux of what I want to share in this chapter. I have come to the conclusion that sin and sickness cannot exist in the kingdom of God. Wherever the kingdom of God is truly established, sin and sickness are banished. They are as incompatible as light and darkness.

In another prophecy about the Messiah from Malachi 4:2, one we have discussed earlier, the Lord says, *"To you who fear My name The Sun of Righteousness shall arise with healing in His wings."* Again, Jesus' light produces two things: righteousness and healing. The opposite of righteousness and healing—sin and sickness—are the works of darkness. The distinction is very clear.

When Jesus first sent out His disciples with the message of the kingdom, He said to them,

Do not go into the way of the Gentiles, and do not enter a city of the Samaritans. But go rather to the lost sheep of the house of Israel. And as you go, preach [proclaim], saying, "The

kingdom of heaven is at hand."

(Matthew 10:5–7)

Since *"the kingdom of heaven is at hand,"* what should be done?

Heal the sick, cleanse the lepers, raise the dead, cast out demons. (verse 8)

What does that string of commands represent? It is the proof of the kingdom. God has never expected the world to believe the message without the proof, and the church has never been authorized to offer the message without the proof. Where there is no proof, there really isn't any kingdom. There is just a theological abstraction.

In Matthew 12:28, Jesus indicated this truth in just one simple statement:

If I cast out demons by the Spirit of God, surely the kingdom of God has come upon you.

Jesus talked about the clash of the two invisible kingdoms—the kingdom of light, which is the kingdom of God, and the kingdom of darkness, which is the kingdom of Satan. The driving out of demons by the authority of Jesus Christ brings the two kingdoms into focus and demonstrates the victory of the kingdom of light over the kingdom of darkness. That is the proof.

The Prayer of the Kingdom

Now, we come to the *prayer* of the kingdom, which is often called the Lord's Prayer. In Matthew 6, Jesus instructed His disciples how to pray:

In this manner, therefore, pray: Our Father in heaven, hallowed be Your name.

(Matthew 6:9)

The first part of the prayer provides the address and the attitude of reverence with which we must approach God the Father. Next, what is the first petition, or priority number one?

Your kingdom come. (verse 10)

Directly associated with that priority is:

Your will be done on earth as it is in heaven.

(verse 10)

> **The purpose of the gospel is not to get us to heaven but to get heaven to earth.**

Where is the kingdom to come? On earth. Most Christians have the idea that the purpose of the gospel is to get us to heaven. That is not so. The purpose of the gospel is to get heaven to earth. This is what we ask for every time we pray the Lord's Prayer. If we don't believe that, we shouldn't pray it—otherwise, we are hypocrites. Let me ask you a simple

96

question. Do you believe that God's will can be done on earth to the same extent that it is done in heaven? If you don't believe that, don't pray it.

All other prayers are secondary to this prayer for the coming of God's kingdom. In other words, all our personal needs, desires, and problems have to take second place to the coming of the kingdom of God. My opinion is that probably 90 percent of the professing Christian church today is not in that relationship to God—and I think that may be a very conservative estimate. Most Christians put their own wants, their own needs, and their own problems before the coming of the kingdom of God. They have put the cart before the horse.

The Priority of the Kingdom

The final phase is the *priority* of the kingdom, which is very closely related to the prayer of the kingdom. It is also found in Matthew 6:

> *But seek first the kingdom of God and His righteousness, and all these things* [all your material and physical needs] *shall be added to you.*
> (Matthew 6:33)

This command helps us to keep our priorities right. Again, the kingdom of God comes before all our personal needs and problems.

THE ADMINISTRATOR OF THE KINGDOM

If we will respond properly to the message of the kingdom, we will see its effects in a practical way in our lives and in our physical bodies. To put this truth in context, we need to examine Jesus' statement in Luke 17:

> *Now when* [Jesus] *was asked by the Pharisees when the kingdom of God would come, He answered them and said, "The kingdom of God does not come with observation* ["does not come visibly" NIV]; *nor will they say, 'See here!' or 'See there!' For indeed, the kingdom of God is within you."* (Luke 17:20–21)

The kingdom that Jesus was talking about is first and foremost invisible and internal. That is not to say that the kingdom of God will never be visibly established. But, at the present time, it is not a visible, material, earthly kingdom. It is an invisible, inward, spiritual kingdom. The nature of this kingdom was stated by Paul in one verse:

> *For the kingdom of God is not eating and drinking, but* [It's not a question of what you eat or drink, or don't eat or drink, but three things:]

righteousness and peace and joy in the Holy Spirit. (Romans 14:17)

What comes first? Righteousness. Why? Jesus said, *"Seek first the kingdom of God and His righteousness"* (Matthew 6:33, emphasis added). The Bible makes it very clear that outside of the kingdom of God, there is no righteousness. Everybody who is not under the kingship of Jesus is a rebel. You can be very religious and pious but still be a rebel. And rebels have no righteousness, no peace, and no joy.

> **The kingdom of God, under the kingship of Jesus, is righteousness, peace, and joy.**

I was preaching on this subject once in Lakeland, Florida. A young woman was there who had been brought up as a Pentecostal from infancy, but she was sick. She had a spot on her lung. As she heard me teaching, the Holy Spirit convicted her. "You're Pentecostal, but you're a rebel." And she repented.

The kingdom of God, then, under the kingship of Jesus, is righteousness; and, following that, it is peace. If your heart and life are in turmoil today, you should check your spiritual condition. Peace is the result of righteousness. Next is joy. The majority of Christians may be pursuing peace and joy, but, in many cases, they are bypassing righteousness. That is a dead end. It won't get you where you want to go. You take care of the righteousness and let God the Father take care of the peace and the joy.

Notice one more vital factor. It is *"in the Holy Spirit"* (Romans 14:17). Only where the Holy Spirit operates can all this be possible. The only administrator of the kingdom is the Holy Spirit. It is not a denomination. It is not a doctrine. It is a spiritual reality. Many people have all the language, but without the Holy Spirit, nothing works. Only where the Holy Spirit is operating will the kingdom of God work.

PHYSICAL IMPLICATIONS OF THE KINGDOM MESSAGE

I want to close this chapter by sharing how the kingdom message can impact us physically in the area of healing.

One of the problems I experienced in the particular ministry God gave me was tension. I thought to myself, *God must have an answer for tension. If the kingdom of God is a reality, then wherever it is established, there won't be tension, because the kingdom is peace.* I don't claim to have the whole answer, but what I have, I'll share with you.

My area of tension was in my digestive system. I think the problem went back fifty or sixty years. You can have a problem for so long that you think it is a part of yourself. But, I decided that if the kingdom of God ruled in my digestive system, I would not have tension. And how does the kingdom of God come to us? I saw that the kingdom of God comes only by the Holy Spirit. There is no other way.

Let me ask you a question. Would you dare to invite the Holy Spirit into your colon? The marvelous thing about God is that He's so humble, He'll come anyplace you invite Him. Again, you can be so used to having a certain physical condition that you cannot even imagine what it would be like to live without it. That was my experience. Yet I had a dramatic change when I simply said, "God, I give my digestive system over to You. I want the Holy Spirit in control of every area." What I have shared is just a little practical application so you can understand that I'm not teaching theory. To the best of my ability, I am dealing with reality in a very practical way.

I want to share one more personal experience. Once, as I was walking out the door of our condominium, the Lord spoke to me. I wasn't being very spiritual. I wasn't thinking about anything in particular. My mind was in neutral, which can be a time when God speaks to you. Between the time I opened the door to go out and closed the door behind me, God said this to me: "If you will follow the right lifestyle, you can be completely well."

In the next chapter, we will discuss first the healing methods of Jesus and then this concept of the kingdom lifestyle.

Chapter Seven

Healing Methods of Jesus

HOW DID JESUS HEAL?

Jesus Healed People in Crowds Who Followed Him

I believe most of us have a very incomplete picture of the ministry of Jesus when it comes to healing. We envision Him healing people mainly on an individual basis. He certainly did this, but He also often healed large numbers of people at the same time. What Jesus did was to choose a place and a time, get everybody who wanted healing there, and do the job from beginning to end. In many cases, He required people to follow Him for several days before He ministered to their physical needs.

The following are some clear examples of this method of ministry employed by Jesus. The first is in Matthew 12:14–15:

Then the Pharisees went out and plotted against [Jesus], how they might destroy Him. But when Jesus knew it, He withdrew from there. And

*great multitudes followed Him, and He healed
them all.*

Whom did Jesus heal? The multitudes. But what
had they done first? They had followed Him. They
were not healed where they were. They had to move
out to an unknown destination, following Him until
He chose to stop and begin the ministry of healing.

*Jesus Healed People Who Had
No Other Options*

Next, let's look at the first part of a passage
from Matthew 15:

Jesus departed from [Tyre and Sidon], *skirted
the Sea of Galilee, and went up on the mountain and sat down there. Then great multitudes
came to Him* [at the top of the mountain], *having with them the lame, blind, mute, maimed,
and many others; and they laid them down at
Jesus' feet, and He healed them.*

(Matthew 15:29–30)

Imagine carrying a paralyzed person up a mountain! You either had faith by the time you got to the
top, or you didn't get there. Then, the passage says:

*So the multitude marveled when they saw the
mute speaking, the maimed made whole, the
lame walking, and the blind seeing; and they*

glorified the God of Israel. Now Jesus called His disciples to Himself and said, "I have compassion on the multitude, because they have now continued with Me three days and have nothing to eat." (Matthew 15:31–32)

Jesus had conducted a three-day healing service, and there was no refreshment. Please understand that we are talking about a totally different level of commitment. I can understand this very well, having ministered in the Third World. The people didn't have any options. There were no hospitals. There was no malaria medicine. There was no vaccine against typhus or measles. Their options were minimal. It was either Jesus or nothing.

Similarly, in Matthew 19, we discover an answer to the question, "Why do so many people get healed in Third World nations?" One of the reasons is that they have no options, much like the crowds in Jesus' day.

Now it came to pass, when Jesus had finished these sayings, that He departed from Galilee and came to the region of Judea beyond the · Jordan [a journey of two or three days on foot]. And great multitudes followed Him, and He healed them there. (Matthew 19:1–2)

Where did Jesus heal the people? *"There"*—at the *end* of the two- or three-day journey. Do you

105

understand this point? These verses give us a totally different picture of the healing ministry of Jesus from the one we usually have.

On one of our trips to a Third World nation, my wife, Ruth, and I got into what I would call mass healing—not by choice, but simply under pressure. It was the only practical way we could minister healing. As I was thinking how very eccentric and unorthodox it was, God opened my eyes to see that this was the way Jesus did it.

One other factor is that when you become focused on healing, and that is what you are going to do, there is a different attitude in everybody. When we would have a healing service, I would tell people that the purpose of the service was just one thing—healing. We would be just as practical as a doctor or a dentist. It was simply that we would use different methods.

I thought mass healing was unorthodox, but God opened my eyes to see that this was the way Jesus did it.

Often, I would say, "Ruth and I will stay here as long as our strength lasts." One interesting thing we always noticed was that if we had been ministering for five or six hours in a service, we would see two things happen in the last hour. First, there would be a number of outstanding miracles, because people would be desperate. Second, nearly always, a number of young men would come up for prayer at the end. Often, they had been too shy and had held back out of sensitivity and a desire to be inconspicuous. We saw those two events as a recurring principle.

Jesus Healed Those Whose Hearts Cried Out to God

Against that background, I want to relate one last incident from Matthew 15 that provides another dimension to Jesus' healing ministry.

Then Jesus went out from there [the region of Galilee] *and departed to the region of Tyre and Sidon.*   (Matthew 15:21)

Jesus had been to Galilee, and then He went to Tyre and Sidon. We have already seen that the return journey must have taken three or four days. So, Jesus went from Galilee to Tyre and then back from Tyre to Galilee. The New Testament records only one thing that He did in Tyre. One thing only. There is no reason to believe He did anything else. What we find is that Jesus gave more than one week of His ministry for the sake of one woman—a woman we have met before. Let's read the whole passage.

Then Jesus went out from there and departed to the region of Tyre and Sidon. And behold, a woman of Canaan came from that region and cried out to Him, saying, "Have mercy on me, O Lord, Son of David! My daughter is severely demon-possessed." But He answered her not a word. And His disciples came and urged Him, saying, "Send her away, for she cries out after us." But He answered and said, "I was not sent except to the lost sheep of the house of Israel." Then she came and worshiped Him, saying, "Lord, help me!" [Brief prayers are sometimes the best.] *But He answered and said, "It is not good to take the children's bread and throw it to the little dogs." And she said, "Yes, Lord, yet even the little dogs eat the crumbs which fall from their masters' table." The Jesus answered and said to her, "O woman, great is your faith! Let it be to you as you desire." And her daughter was healed from that very hour.*

(Matthew 15:21–28)

It is helpful for us to see that Jesus did not heal only the masses. It is clear from this passage that He would spend a week of His precious ministry to go and visit one non-Jewish woman. What got Him there? The story doesn't tell us, so I will just give you my opinion. I have learned in my ministry that there is such a thing as the cry to God of a desperate heart. I believe that cry never goes unanswered.

Often, I would find myself in places where I said, "God, how did I ever get here?" The conclusion I came to on such occasions was that there was a heart crying out to God that would not be denied. God will change all of history to meet a person like that at the point of ministry. Isn't He wonderful?

Having examined the ministry of Jesus and the methods He used in healing as He brought the kingdom of God to earth, I now want to share the personal implications of the kingdom in our lives, especially in relation to healing.

ESTABLISHING THE KINGDOM: NO SICKNESS OR REBELLION

I wrote at the end of the previous chapter that God told me I could be completely well as a reflection of His kingdom in my life. It was an appealing thought, as well as one that really makes sense to me. At that time, I was already meditating on such truths about the kingdom of God, and I happened to discover two verses in Isaiah 33 that expressed them as well as any verses I know. They are a prophetic

> *God told me I could be completely well as a reflection of His kingdom in my life.*

picture of the kingdom established on earth. It has
not yet been fully established on earth, but I believe
it is going to be. The principles are true already, and
I am going to present them here.

*For the LORD is our Judge, the LORD is our
Lawgiver, the LORD is our King; He will save
us.*   (Isaiah 33:22)

I believe the above verse is a description of salvation. When you can say those three things about the
Lord and make it personal—the Lord is my Judge,
the Lord is my Lawgiver, the Lord is my King—you
have salvation. Now, in verse 24, we see the results
of that salvation:

*And the inhabitant will not say, "I am sick";
the people who dwell in it will be forgiven their
iniquity* [rebellion].   (verse 24)

What are the results of the kingdom being established in your life? No sickness and no rebellion.
It is totally logical, if you stop to think about it. It
could not be otherwise. On the basis of what we have
learned about the kingdom of God, it has to be that
way.

Let's first take a moment to consider what is involved in these statements: the Lord is my Judge,
the Lord is my Lawgiver, the Lord is my King.

The Lord Is My Judge

When we say, "The Lord is my Judge," what we are really saying is, "Lord, You tell me what's right and wrong. It's not my decision to make; it's Yours. If You say a thing is wrong, it's wrong, no matter what I think about it." Are you open to God's judgment on your life, or are you afraid of it?

I will give you a very down-to-earth example of God being the Judge in our lives. Some years ago, I went to see a movie called *The Frisco Kid*, which I thought was one of the best and funniest movies I'd ever seen. I enjoyed it especially because it had a Jewish theme to it. I don't want to put a guilt trip on anybody, but as much as I liked it, I decided not to see it again because of the language in it. The foul language in it is totally unnecessary, and it makes no difference to the story whatever. But I did not feel free to put the Holy Spirit in me in the presence of that language.

If you let the Lord be your Judge, you may be shocked at how it alters your behavior. There are two guiding principles in the Bible that help in this regard: (1) Whatever you do, do it to the glory of God (see 1 Corinthians 10:31), and (2) Whatever you do, do it in the name of the Lord Jesus Christ (see Colossians 3:17). You are not free, biblically, to do anything that you cannot do to the glory of God and in the name of the Lord Jesus Christ. I am not interested in, nor do I have enough time to waste on, formalities and religiosity. I am interested in reality, and the Lord being my Judge.

The Lord Is My Lawgiver

The next statement is where the shoe really begins to pinch: "The Lord is my Lawgiver." Based on Old Testament Hebrew, I interpret this declaration to mean that the Lord sets my lifestyle. I believe that is exactly what it means. Please answer honestly: Does the Lord set your lifestyle? You can have a religious lifestyle in which you don't drink certain drinks and don't go to certain places of entertainment. Yet that is not the reality of a kingdom lifestyle. I have lived through all of that. I know all the taboos. I have even taught them! They are sheer legalism, and legalism has nothing to do with what I am talking about.

> **"The Lord is my Lawgiver" means that the Lord sets my lifestyle.**

Our lifestyles are built around three things that are not overtly spiritual: diet, exercise, and rest. I have come to the conclusion that you cannot expect to be healthy and functioning effectively if you ignore any of those three areas. For example, you can fill your stomach with junk food, but, sooner or later, your stomach is going to rebel. It may take twenty or thirty years, but it will catch up with you. The same is true if you mistreat other areas of your body.

When I had a problem with potential skin cancer, I went to a wonderful dermatologist in Florida who became a close friend of mine. One thing he told me was that most of us got all the sun we needed twenty-five years ago. When he said that, I did a little mental calculation. Where was I twenty-five years ago? I was living right on the equator. And I was so proud of myself that I didn't have to wear a hat. Twenty-five years later, it caught up with me.

When a little problem arose, I went to an orthodox Jewish dermatologist in Jerusalem. He asked me, "Were you a sun worshipper?" I thought for a moment, and I had to admit I had been. He said, "Thou shalt have no other gods but Me," and hit the nail right on the head. (See Exodus 20:3.) When people expose their skin day after day to the sun, I know where it ends. Even if you don't get skin cancer, when you're fifty or sixty, you will look like a worn leather bag.

Regarding diet and exercise, you may be able to get away with bad habits for forty years, but, at some point, your tight belt will start to tell you something is wrong. That's the first warning. When I was younger, I could eat anything and never get fat. Then, in my mid-forties, I noticed something was changing. When I was in Denmark in 1962, the Lord got me alone on a cliff top. He reminded me of all the things I had achieved and where I was, and then He said, "Are you satisfied, or do you want to go further?"

That was a shock to me because, at that point (I'm ashamed to say), I didn't think there was any further to go. After all, I was baptized in the Spirit, I preached, I ministered, I spoke in tongues, I believed in the second coming of Jesus Christ, and so on. The Lord's question set me back so much that, for three days, I did not give Him an answer. Then I hiked back up to the top of the cliff and said, "Lord, I'm ready to answer You now. I'm not satisfied." When I said that, I realized for the first time how dissatisfied I really was (and how dissatisfied most Christian ministers are).

So, I said, "Lord, I'm not satisfied. If there is anything further, I want to go further." The Lord gave me an immediate answer: "There are two conditions. First of all, all progress in the Christian life is by faith. Second, you're putting on too much weight! If you want to fulfill the ministry that I have for you, you'll have to see to that. You'll need a strong, healthy body."

Years later, reflecting on the physically taxing ministry the Lord opened up to me, I just say, "Thank You, Lord. You warned me in time." After that warning, I basically kept a careful check on my weight. But it wouldn't have been that way if the Lord had not caught me at age forty-seven and warned me.

The third thing I want to mention is rest. Ultimately, rest is as important as diet or exercise. And here is where most active Christians are out of line with God. Which do you think takes more faith—to work or to rest? The answer is rest. If you can only work, you are lacking in faith. I try to rest when the Lord tells me to rest. This doesn't mean I follow a legalistic observance of the Sabbath, since I live in the freedom provided by Christ. But I find that if I will take the rest God ordains for me—whatever day or time that might be—I will accomplish much more in the remaining periods of work than I will if I am working all the time. It shouldn't be necessary to tell this principle to modern Christians, but it is.

> *To align your lifestyle with the kingdom of God, pray, "Lord, You arrange my diet, my exercise, and my rest."*

If you are going to say, "The Lord is my Lawgiver," you are also going to have to say, "Lord, You arrange my diet, my exercise, and my rest." Are you prepared to do that? It will probably mean radical changes for you.

The Lord Is My King

The last designation is "The Lord is my King." That means you say, "God, whatever You tell me, I'll do. You are my Director." This is very important because it is not a religious system. If the Lord tells you to live in Fort Lauderdale, you cannot be righteous in Miami. You can follow all the rules, attend church, pay your tithe, do all of it, but you are not righteous. If being righteous meant just following a religious system, it wouldn't make any difference. But when it comes to a personal relationship with God as your King, it matters where you are. I have seen in counseling people that many people do not prosper as Christians simply because they are in the wrong geographic location. Do you believe God has a geographic place for you? I do.

To wrap up our discussion of lifestyle, let's look at Luke 5:36:

Then [Jesus] *spoke a parable to them: "No one puts a piece from a new garment on an old one; otherwise the new makes a tear, and also the piece that was taken out of the new does not match the old."*

This is a simple, practical parable. In trying to repair a garment, nobody takes a new patch and just sews it over the old material. But, in my opinion, that is the way most Christians face their problems. They say, "God, I've got a tear here. Give me a patch, a little piece of Your supernatural help, and I'll put it on. But don't ask me to change my lifestyle. Don't ask me to put on a totally new garment."

I have been convinced of this as I have seen people come to healing meetings. After listening to all sorts of rubbish, watching all sorts of unedifying shows on television, spending hours on the phone gossiping with their friends, they come and sit in the healing meeting. How can you change all that is in their backgrounds in a short period of time, especially if they are going to go out and live in the same ways again? All they are asking from God is a little patch of His supernatural power and blessing on their old garments.

I have come to the conclusion that God is not going to be dealing with us in that way much longer. I am amazed at the grace that He shows people. Yet, if I understand correctly, God may have closed His eyes to this ignorance in the past, but He's now commanding everybody everywhere to repent. (See Acts 17:30–31.) May God help you to live out your days. May He allow you to fulfill your appointed span. It will take applying what I have shared in this chapter. Do you believe that is true? If so, you need to take action on it.

ARE YOU WILLING?

The kingdom of God is a "social security" kingdom. When you are in it, everything is included. God has made provision for all your needs. (See, for example, John 10:10; 16:24.) What I am going to suggest, after you ponder it for a moment, is that you pray, "God, I am willing for You to be my Judge, my Lawgiver, and my King. You tell me what's right and wrong in my life. You set my lifestyle, and I'll obey Your orders."

> **The kingdom of God is a "social security" kingdom. God has made provision for all your needs.**

Don't worry about doing this perfectly. I'm just asking if you would like to make this your goal. Would you say, "Lord, I will say this today because I would like You to make it true in my life"? If you would like to do that, I suggest that you repeat the prayer below in a sincere way, beginning with a declaration of faith.

This is a serious commitment. I want you to know that in advance because it is going to change a lot of things in your life. But the changes will all be for the better. Are you ready to follow Jesus completely, as the multitudes of His day did, who had no other options? Are you ready to exchange your lifestyle for the kingdom lifestyle? Then, please pray this prayer:

Lord Jesus Christ, I believe that You are the Son of God and the only way to God. You died on the cross for my sins and rose again from the dead. I want You to be my Judge, my Lawgiver, and my King, from this day forward. I want to be fully in Your kingdom and under Your authority. In Jesus' name I pray, amen.

If you are serious about this commitment, then please repeat the prayer once more.

Chapter Eight

Healing as a Gift of the Spirit

O ne of the key passages we have referred to in our exploration of the topic of healing is Acts 4:29–30. This passage is part of a prayer that the early disciples prayed, and it is one that we ought to pray, as well, as we ask God to pour out His healing power in our day.

THAT POWERFUL PRAYER

Remember that in the formative days of the early church, the apostles were forbidden to preach any longer in the name of Jesus. (See Acts 4:18.) The religious and political opposition had focused on that one vital aspect of their ministry.

As I wrote earlier, I do not doubt that Satan inspired those officials to make that decision, because by trying to withhold from the early Christians the right to use the name of Jesus, they were attempting to remove the entire power and authority of the gospel. Every promise and every provision of God is available only through the name of Jesus—whether it be forgiveness of sins, eternal life, healing of sickness, deliverance from evil spirits, holiness, or anything else. (See John 14:12–14; 15:16; 16:23–24.)

How did the church confront this tremendous crisis? Having been told not to preach any longer in the name of Jesus, they went to prayer. Scripture tells us they gathered together and lifted up their voices with one accord and prayed the prayer in Acts 4. We will not go through the whole prayer here, but we will focus on the last two verses of it.

Again, I believe this prayer is sanctioned and approved by God. First of all, it was prayed together in unison by the apostles and the rest of the early church. Second, the Holy Spirit caused it to be recorded in Scripture. I believe it is still a very good prayer and that it continues to represent the mind and will of God today.

As we did in chapter one, let us read part of the prayer from Acts 4. I urge you to make it your personal prayer and commitment for healing power to burst forth in your life.

Now, Lord, look on their threats, and grant to Your servants that with all boldness they may speak Your word, by stretching out Your hand to heal, and that signs and wonders may be done through the name of Your holy Servant Jesus. (Acts 4:29–30)

When you dare to be specific, God gives His attention to your prayers.

Did you pray that prayer? Would you dare to be specific enough to ask God to fulfill it today? Would you dare to pray that He will do the things that are stated in that verse in very definite ways in your life? When you dare to be specific, God gives His attention to your prayers.

The results of this prayer in the ministry of Jesus' disciples were powerful:

When they had prayed, the place where they were assembled together was shaken; and they were all filled with the Holy Spirit, and they spoke the word of God with boldness....And through the hands of the apostles many signs and wonders were done among the people.... And believers were increasingly added to the Lord, multitudes of both men and women, so that they brought the sick out into the streets and laid them on beds and couches, that at least the shadow of Peter passing by might fall on some of them. Also a multitude gathered from the surrounding cities to Jerusalem, bringing sick people and those who were tormented by

unclean spirits, and they were all healed.
                        (Acts 4:31; 5:12, 14–16)

Notice that the disciples were all filled with the Holy Spirit, who enabled them to preach the Word of God with boldness, and through whom they brought healing and deliverance to the people. Again, we see the Word of God attested by signs and wonders. We must realize that healing ministry means allowing the Holy Spirit to bring the evidence of the kingdom of God through us.

GIFTS OF THE HOLY SPIRIT

The gifts of the Holy Spirit are one of the ways through which the Holy Spirit administers the riches of God's kingdom through Christ. They are not the only way, but they are one way this happens, and it will be helpful for us to discuss the ministry of healing and our personal involvement in it in the context of these gifts.

I'm going to teach very briefly on the gifts of the Spirit and then provide some application to those gifts specifically dealing with healing and miracles. It is not my purpose to dwell extensively on any of the other gifts, although they are important, because that would take many chapters of teaching, and our emphasis is on healing. To begin, let's look at what Paul wrote in the twelfth chapter of 1 Corinthians:

> *But the manifestation of the Spirit is given to each one* [individually] *for the profit of all.*
>
> (1 Corinthians 12:7)

The manifestations of the Holy Spirit are available to every believer. (See also 1 Corinthians 12:31; 14:1.) No believer should be without the manifestations of the Spirit. They are given for a useful, practical, beneficial purpose—to do good. As my friend Bob Mumford has often said, "The gifts of the Holy Spirit are not toys; they're tools. And without the tools, you can't do the job." Here, then, are the gifts:

> *For to one is given the word of wisdom through the Spirit, to another the word of knowledge through the same Spirit, to another faith by the same Spirit, to another gifts of healings by the same Spirit, to another the working of miracles, to another prophecy, to another discerning of spirits, to another different kinds of tongues, to another the interpretation of tongues. But one and the same Spirit works all these things, distributing to each one individually as He wills.*
>
> (1 Corinthians 12:8–11)

At both the beginning and the end of that list, Paul emphasized that these gifts or manifestations of the Holy Spirit are for each believer individually. No believer needs to be without his own specific, God-appointed manifestations of the Holy Spirit. If you are living without the gifts and the manifestations of the Holy Spirit in your life, you are living below the revealed will of God the Father for you as a believer in Jesus Christ and as a member of Christ's body. It is not the will of God that any believer be without the enjoyment and use of these gifts.

> *No believer needs to be without his own specific, God-appointed manifestations of the Holy Spirit.*

An Overview of the Gifts

In the above passage, nine gifts are listed, and they may be conveniently divided into three categories, with three gifts in each category. Many well-known Bible teachers have pointed this out. We will look briefly at the three categories and the three gifts that belong in each category.

The first category we will call the gifts of revelation.

The second category we will call the vocal gifts.

The third category we will call the power gifts (for lack of a better word).

THE GIFTS OF REVELATION

Let's begin with the gifts of revelation. The first gift listed is *a word of wisdom*. Where the *New King James Version* says "the" word of wisdom, the original Greek says "a" word of wisdom. I think it is better put that way. God has all wisdom, but, fortunately for you and me, He doesn't dump it all out on us in one outpouring. If He were to do so, we would be submerged. However, every now and then, when we are moving in the will of God and need wisdom that is not available to us by natural means, at that point, the Holy Spirit will supernaturally impart to us a word of divine wisdom.

> **Knowledge gives you information; wisdom tells you what to do with it.**

The next gift listed is *a word of knowledge*. Again, the original Greek is "a" rather than "the" word of knowledge. The difference between knowledge and wisdom is important. *Knowledge* is informative; *wisdom* is directive. Ecclesiastes 10:10 says, *"Wisdom is profitable to direct"*

(KJV). Knowledge gives you information; wisdom tells you what to do with it.

Some people have a lot of knowledge but no wisdom with which to use it. We need both, and we really need them combined. You may have much wisdom, but if you do not have the facts, you have nothing to act on. Sometimes, you need specific knowledge. You are walking in the purposes of God, doing the will of God, and you come to a place where you need knowledge not available to you by any natural means. At that point, the Holy Spirit of God will supernaturally impart to you a word of knowledge—again, just a tiny seed of the total knowledge of God.

The third gift of revelation is *discernings of spirits*. In the original Greek, both parts of this phrase are plural. Rather than "discerning" of spirits, it is "discernings" of spirits. About five of these gifts are plural in both parts. I believe every discerning is a gift. In other words, every time you are able to discern, it is an individual gift. That is why the gift is collectively discernings of spirits.

To discern is to recognize and to distinguish between. For example, you recognize and distinguish between the various kinds of spirits that confront you in the Christian life. There are many. There is the Holy Spirit, and it is very important to discern the Holy Spirit. Some people fail to discern the Holy

Spirit—they don't recognize Him when He is at work. They sometimes dismiss Him. The manifestations of the Holy Spirit are sometimes very unexpected. There have been groups that have prayed for the Holy Spirit to come, and when He came, He came in such a way that they did not recognize Him, so they refused Him.

There are angelic spirits—good angels and evil angels. Discernings of spirits deals with both categories. In Acts 27, when Paul was on a ship in a severe storm, an angel of God visited the ship. Apparently, the only person who knew the angel was there was Paul. Nobody else discerned the angel's presence.

Then, there is the discerning of demons or evil spirits. There are many categories of evil spirits. Sometimes, we need to be able to discern between those categories or just recognize an evil spirit. Many times, evil spirits will seek to counterfeit the Holy Spirit—which has been one of the problems of certain movements. Some Christians have been taken in by counterfeits, and those believers have attributed to the Holy Spirit what actually has been the work of evil spirits. They have done so unknowingly, unintentionally, but through lack of discernment. So, we need to be able to discern the presence and activity and operation of evil spirits.

Then, there is the human spirit, which is distinct from all the others. Jesus discerned in Nathanael a guileless spirit. (See John 1:47 KJV.) These are some of the ways that discernings of spirits can operate in Christian practice.

THE VOCAL GIFTS

We move on now to the vocal gifts. The first one is *prophecy*, which is an utterance given by the Holy Spirit through a person in a language understood by the person speaking and understood by those who are spoken to. Prophecy is not inspired preaching. It is a supernatural manifestation of the Holy Spirit.

The next gift in the vocal list is *kinds of tongues*. In the King James Version, it is called *"divers kinds of tongues"* (1 Corinthians 12:10) or *"diversities of tongues"* (1 Corinthians 12:28), but the Greek is identical in both verses. Notice, again, that both parts are plural: kinds of tongues.

As I understand it, this gift does not refer to the *"unknown tongue"* with which believers communicate with God in their personal devotions. (See, for example, 1 Corinthians 14:2 KJV.) This is a public ministry in the assembly, and there are various kinds of tongues. Not various different languages, but various uses or functions of tongues in public. I will offer you four without commenting on them: intercession, praise, rebuke, and exhortation. If the message in an unknown tongue is an exhortation, then it must be interpreted in a known language to be effective.

The third gift under this heading is *interpretation*, which I understand to be interpretation of tongues.[1]

THE POWER GIFTS

Power Gift #1: Faith

The last group of three is the power gifts. The first of these gifts is *faith*. I want to point out that various kinds of faith are spoken about in the New Testament.

First of all, there is what I call "faith to live by." Romans 1:17 says, *"The just shall live by faith."* Every believer has to have that kind of faith—faith he lives by. Your whole life as a Christian is based on faith in Jesus Christ and the Word of God. That kind of faith comes in the Romans 10:17 way: *"So then faith comes by hearing, and hearing by the word of God."*

Then, there is faith that is a fruit of the Holy Spirit. The fruit of the Holy Spirit is listed in Galatians 5:22–23. The ninefold fruit of the Spirit, in the wording of the King James Version, is *"love, joy, peace,*

---

[1]For further teaching on this theme, see Derek Prince, *The Gifts of the Spirit* (New Kensington, PA: Whitaker House, 2007).

longsuffering, gentleness, goodness, faith, meekness, temperance." Number seven in that list is faith. Fruit relates to character. The fruit of the Spirit represents various aspects of total Christian character. And fruit has to be cultivated—it does not come by an instantaneous act.

We can see the difference between the gift of faith and the fruit of faith very clearly when we consider the difference between a Christmas tree and an apple tree. A Christmas tree has ornaments and gifts on it. An apple tree bears fruit. You can put a gift on a Christmas tree by an instantaneous act and remove it by an instantaneous act. That is how the gifts of the Spirit are received—instantaneously. But you don't put an apple on an apple tree by an instantaneous act. It grows by a process. If it is going to be worth eating, it has to be cultivated. That is Christian character—the fruit of the Spirit. It comes by a process. In the business world, you cannot market uncultivated fruit, and God is not interested in uncultivated fruit, either.

The fruit of faith is an aspect of Christian character. I define it as a quiet, steady, continuing trust that doesn't get shaken, doesn't get upset, doesn't get disturbed. I am sure you will agree that type of faith has to be cultivated. It cannot happen in five minutes. But when you have been through fifteen crises already, and you remain steady and unmoved in the sixteenth

131

one, knowing that God is still in control, then that, I believe, is the manifestation of the fruit of faith.

In contrast, the gift of faith is supernatural faith. It is God's own faith. This gift is very similar to a word of wisdom and a word of knowledge. Remember that we said the gifts of wisdom and knowledge represent just a little bit of God's wisdom and a little bit of God's knowledge. Likewise, the gift of faith is just a little bit of God's faith imparted supernaturally to you. Everything God has ever done, He has done by faith. God created the universe by faith. By His own word, *"He spoke, and it was done; He commanded, and it stood fast"* (Psalm 33:9). Faith is divine, creative, and irresistible.

> **The gift of faith is a little mustard seed of divine faith dropped into your heart. And while you have it, you are just as effective as God Himself.**

At one point, Jesus cursed a fig tree, and within twenty-four hours, it had withered from the roots. He didn't lay hands on the fig tree, He didn't anoint the fig tree, He just spoke to the fig tree. When Peter commented on the fact that the fig tree was withered in twenty-four hours, Jesus said to His disciples, "Have the faith of God." (See Mark 11:22.) That is the correct translation: "Have the faith of God." Have God's faith. That is what we are talking about in the gift of faith. It is a little mustard seed of divine faith dropped into your heart. And while you have it, you are just as effective as God Himself. It doesn't matter whether God speaks to the fig tree or you speak to the fig tree—it will have to wither because it is God's faith that enables you to speak.

In this connection, it isn't the quantity of faith that matters but the quality. Jesus said all you need is faith the size of a mustard seed to move a mountain. (See Matthew 17:20.) You can speak to the mountain. In most cases, this faith operates through a spoken word, as God's faith did. *"He spoke, and it was done; He commanded, and it stood fast."* He said, *"'Let there be light'; and there was light"* (Genesis 1:3). That is God's faith. While you have it, you are irresistible. When God's faith leaves, you are back again to your own human abilities. The gift of faith is usually just a brief impartation of a little divine faith for a specific purpose that God wants accomplished.

Power Gifts #2 and #3: Healings and Miracles

Now we come to the other two gifts of power, and it will be helpful to consider them together: *gifts of healings* and *workings of miracles*. Notice again that both parts are plural in each of these

Each healing is a gift and each miracle is a working.

133

two gifts. Gifts of healings and workings of miracles. My personal impression is that each healing is a gift and each miracle is a working. Every time a healing comes, it is a gift.

It is important for us to understand the relationship between healings and miracles. Essentially, healings relate to sicknesses. If there is sickness in a body, then the healing power of God by the operation of a gift deals with that condition of sickness, removes the sickness, and replaces it with health. Healings are frequently invisible. They are also not always consummated in one single act but are quite often gradual and progressive. The healing power may be at work over a period of time.

On the other hand, miracles go beyond healings. If you have recurrent earaches, the healing power of God may remove the earaches. But if your middle ear has been removed by surgery, so that you have no middle ear, one cannot heal a middle ear that isn't there. But, a creative miracle will restore a middle ear—and I have seen this happen.

To take another example, which is rather controversial, if you have a cavity in your tooth, you can't heal a cavity. But a creative miracle of God will replace the cavity. You may think this sounds strange, but as an honest witness in a court of law, I would have to testify that I have seen it happen. I once watched while a dark cavity filled up with yellow gold in approximately sixty seconds—with no human intervention. I watched the whole process inside a person's mouth from beginning to end. That is a miracle. I hope you would agree with that!

Years ago, I met a Lutheran woman in Minneapolis who said, "The Lord filled my tooth." When she told me her testimony, I asked, "Would you mind letting me look at it?" She pulled her gum back, and the tooth I saw was coated with a kind of porcelain. It was beautiful, and it was contoured to fit the crown of the tooth exactly. I asked, "What did your dentist say?" She replied, "The dentist said, 'We don't use material like that!'" This same woman also had two disintegrated vertebrae in her neck that God totally restored. Those were two creative miracles—one in her tooth and one in her neck.

MINISTRIES APPOINTED IN THE CHURCH

Having covered the gifts listed in 1 Corinthians 12:7–11, let's move on to 1 Corinthians 12:28, which lists ministries appointed in the church:

And God has appointed these in the church: first apostles, second prophets, third teachers, after that miracles, then gifts of healings, helps, administrations, varieties of tongues.

In 1 Corinthians 11, 12, and 14, when Paul was writing about *"the church,"* the inference was that he was talking about the official public assembly of God's people. He said that God had appointed some in the church, and he gave a specific order. He mentioned eight ministries in the above verse, the first three being apostles, prophets, and teachers.

Those are the three senior ministries in authority in the assembly. The essential point about them is that they are ministries of the Word. Bear in mind that the Word is the supreme authority in the assembly of God's people. All else is subject to the authority of the Word and must be judged by the standards of the Word.

Miracles and gifts of healings are part of the total provision of God in the assembly of His people.

After apostles, prophets, and teachers, the next two in the list are miracles and gifts of healings. I believe that, if we are in New Testament order, every assembly of God's people properly constituted will include those who exercise the gift of the workings of miracles and those who exercise the gifts of healings. They are part of the total provision of God in the assembly of

His people. The New Testament anticipates that they will always be there.

Ministering the Spirit

For further light on the place of miracles in the church, let us go to Galatians 3:5:

> *He therefore that ministereth to you the Spirit, and worketh miracles among you, doeth he it by the works of the law, or by the hearing of faith?* (KJV)

Paul assumed that in the assembly, there would be at least one person who would do two things. First, he would minister the Holy Spirit, enabling God's people to receive the gift, or baptism, of the Holy Spirit. This is a valid ministry, and I think we greatly need it. I have met people who have been in churches for five or ten years, and they tell me they have been seeking the Holy Spirit. Why? Because there is no one who knows how to minister the Holy Spirit. You should need to seek for only five or ten minutes if you are properly instructed.

One of our problems is that we have started wrong. This is not a criticism; it is just an assessment. Often, the accepted method of getting people baptized in the Spirit is

The divine pattern is to minister the Spirit through the hearing of faith.

137

to preach an emotional type of sermon to build up an atmosphere where people can come forward to the altar. They kneel there and start praying without any instruction. And for every person kneeling, there are about three people behind them squeezing them and laying hands on them and "pumping" the Holy Spirit into them! After a while, amid the babble of voices, you'll hear a person speaking in tongues.

But that is not the divine pattern. The divine pattern is to minister the Spirit through the hearing of faith. In other words, I instruct people on the nature of the gift, the requirements for receiving it, and how to receive it. Then, I lead them in a prayer, they drink in, and they receive it. I very rarely spend more than five minutes praying with people to receive the Holy Spirit. I have often said, "If you're not ready, then come back when you are." That is the aspect of ministering the Spirit.

Working Miracles

The other aspect of ministry Paul wrote about in Galatians 3:5 was the workings of miracles. I want to point out that there is a very real place for this gift in the church today. Paul assumed that in the church's assembly, there would be someone who worked miracles. That person would work miracles in the same way that he ministered the Spirit—by the hearing of faith. We work miracles by the hearing of faith.

Let us look at a rather fascinating word found in Acts 19:11–12.

> *God worked unusual [*"special"* KJV] miracles by the hands of Paul, so that even handkerchiefs or aprons were brought from his body to the sick, and the diseases left them and the evil spirits went out of them.*

Do you know the word that fascinates me? *"Unusual"* or *"special."* Think of the implications of that word. Miracles were normal in the church, but some miracles were *unusual* miracles, some were *special* miracles. That passage always prompts me to ask this question: In your church, how normal are miracles? Miracles were taken for granted in the early church, but the ones recorded in Acts 19 were somewhat special. They were unusual; they went beyond the norm.

We will keep this fact in mind when we come to the testimonies in chapter eleven as I share how the Lord led me into the working of miracles of healing.

Chapter Nine

Invisible Barriers to Healing

I have seen thousands of people healed over the years, but I have also noticed that some of God's choicest children do not receive healing. As we discussed in chapter one, the reason some people are not healed is a mystery known only to God. *"The secret things belong to the LORD our God, but those things which are revealed belong to us and to our children forever, that we may do all the words of this law"* (Deuteronomy 29:29).

The things we can't explain or understand are secret things belonging to God. However, there are other things that are revealed, and they belong to us so that we may receive and act on them. While a lack of healing may sometimes be a mystery, other times, the cause may be identified. It is my responsibility as a teacher of God's Word to minister such revealed things to God's people.

There are certain barriers to healing that we can clearly identify, and which the Holy Spirit will enable us to understand and remove so we can receive the healing Christ has provided for us.

GUIDED BY THE SPIRIT OF TRUTH

One of the titles of the Holy Spirit is the Spirit of Truth. Jesus said,

When He, the Spirit of truth, has come, He will guide you into all truth; for He will not speak on His own authority, but whatever He hears He will speak; and He will tell you things to come. He will glorify Me, for He will take of what is Mine and declare it to you. All things that the Father has are Mine. Therefore I said that He will take of Mine and declare it to you.

(John 16:13–15)

Everything the Father has is invested in the Son. And all the wealth of the Father and the Son is administered by the Holy Spirit. The Spirit is the steward, the keeper of the storehouse. It will be to our benefit to make friends with Him! Let us be open to Him as He teaches us how to receive from that storehouse.

THE BARRIERS ARE NOT ON GOD'S SIDE

In ministering to the sick over the years, I have discovered that any barriers to healing are not on

God's side. When Jesus died, the veil of the temple was torn in two from top to bottom, signifying our access to God through Christ, and every barrier on God's side was removed. (See, for example, Matthew 27:50–51.) Remember, the cross is the meeting place between God and man.

> **The veil of the temple was torn in two, signifying our access to God through Christ.**

Yet I have learned by experience that barriers to healing often remain within the hearts and lives of God's people. Whether you are seeking healing for yourself or for others, you must be aware of these barriers and deal with them first. I have discovered that this saves endless time when ministering healing.

SEVEN BARRIERS TO RECEIVING HEALING

I am going to work systematically through seven common barriers that prevent people from receiving healing. There could be others, but these are ones I have identified.

Let me just say that the process we will be going through in this chapter is a little like when you go to the doctor today. Many years ago, the doctor would just listen to your heart, tap you on the back, and say, "Open your mouth and say, 'Ah.'" Then, he might have given you some pills. That picture is rather simplified, but generally, the doctor made his own diagnosis. Today, when you go to the doctor, he or she often orders blood work and other tests to be sent to the laboratory. Then, the tests come back, and they identify where the specific problem areas are so they can be treated. Spiritually speaking, we are going to submit ourselves to all the tests, so we can identify and eliminate any problems in relation to healing. These seven steps are very practical—just as practical and systematic as a contemporary doctor is.

As we progress through each barrier, we will pray to be forgiven and delivered so that we may be free to receive the grace of God in healing.

Ignorance of God's Word and Will

I am sorry to say that ignorance of God's Word and will is a tremendously common barrier to healing in the church today. Multitudes of Christians do not know the clear, simple truths and teachings of the Bible, the Word of God. In Isaiah 5:13, the Lord says,

Therefore my people have gone into captivity, because they have no knowledge.

No knowledge of God's Word. No knowledge of what was accomplished by the death of Jesus on the cross. Ignorance.

In Hosea 4:6, the Lord says something very similar:

My people are destroyed for lack of knowledge.

In what I have presented throughout this book, I believe I have laid a foundation for knowledge of the Word of God and of God's provision through Christ for healing that should help dispel any ignorance of the Scriptures. Yet, to remove this potential barrier and be released from captivity, let us together confess to God our sin and ignorance—the fact that we haven't sought God, we haven't studied His Word, we haven't taken the time to find out what God is saying in the way we should have. We need to ask God to forgive us. And we need to commit ourselves, as far as it is possible, to seek to know the Word and the will of God. I invite you to say this short prayer with me. Will you say these words?

O God, I acknowledge that, in many ways, I have been ignorant of Your Word and of Your will through my own fault. I confess this as a sin. I repent of it. I ask You to forgive me and to help me seek the truth more diligently from this time forward. In Jesus' name, amen.

Unbelief

The next barrier is somewhat related to the first, and it is also alarmingly common in the church. It is unbelief. In many of our churches, we regard unbelief as a kind of harmless weakness. "Well, I don't believe, but, after all, does God really expect me to?"

The New Testament doesn't call unbelief a harmless weakness; it calls it a sin. When we see this truth, we are ready to get rid of unbelief and to open the way through believing God to receive what He has for us. The following Scripture passage is addressed specifically to Christians:

> Beware, brethren, lest there be in any of you an evil heart of unbelief in departing from the living God; but exhort one another daily, while it is called "Today," lest any of you be hardened through the deceitfulness of sin.
>
> (Hebrews 3:12–13)

Notice that the writer called unbelief *"evil"* and *"sin."* In dealing with these spiritual conditions, we have to replace the negative with the positive. First, we ask the Lord to forgive our unbelief. There is not one of us, myself included, who doesn't need to ask forgiveness for unbelief. We renounce this sin; then, we proclaim our faith very

We renounce unbelief and proclaim our faith in God, Jesus, the Holy Spirit, and the Word of God.

simply. We proclaim our faith in God, in Jesus, in the Holy Spirit, and in the Word of God. Doing this can change the entire atmosphere for healing. From this moment on, there can be an atmosphere of faith.

Let us therefore ask God's forgiveness for our unbelief, and then proclaim our faith.

O God, I come to You in Jesus' name, and I confess my sin of unbelief. I do not try to excuse it but admit that I am responsible for it. I am sorry for it, and I renounce it. I ask You to forgive me, to deliver me from this sin of unbelief, and to impart to me Your faith. I want to make this declaration: I believe in God the Father; I believe in God the Son, Jesus Christ; I believe in God the Holy Spirit; and I believe in the Bible—the true, authoritative Word of God. Lord Jesus, I believe what You said: "God's Word is truth." Amen. (See John 17:17.)

Unconfessed Sin

The third barrier is not in every person's life, but it is in many: unconfessed sin. Proverbs 28:13 lays down a vital principle:

He who covers his sins will not prosper, but whoever confesses and forsakes them will have mercy.

You may try desperately to succeed in life in many ways, but if there is hidden, unforgiven sin in your life, you will not prosper in the way you were meant to. I suspect that in the lives of many of us, there are sins that have not been acknowledged. They have not been confessed, and they have not been repented of. We have covered them up, hidden them away.

In dealing with people about the confession of sin, which is so important, I have discovered that many people think, in effect, *If I don't confess my sins to God, He'll never know about them.* Really, I have found many people who think like this. Let me tell you something: God already knows. When you have told Him the worst about yourself, you haven't shocked Him. He knew it all before you told Him.

God is not asking you to confess in order to find out what you've done. He is asking you to confess because when you do, He can help you. Do you understand? It is for your good; it is not for His information. I often tell young people, "There are things you might never be able to tell your parents because you would be too embarrassed and ashamed. But you can tell God, and He is never embarrassed to hear your confessions. He desires to forgive you and to free you from your sins." Isn't that wonderful?

Right now, let's take the opportunity, in the presence of the Holy Spirit, to see if there is any unconfessed sin in our hearts and lives. Let God show you if there is something that you have done or said that was wrong but which you have never dealt with. It may have occurred some years ago, but the Holy Spirit will bring it to your remembrance.

Then, very simply, confess any sin that the Holy Spirit shows you. Respond by saying, "God, I acknowledge this sin. I'm sorry, and I turn away from it. Forgive me and cleanse me in the blood of Jesus." The Bible says, *"If we confess our sins, He is faithful and just to forgive us our sins and to cleanse us from all unrighteousness"* (1 John 1:9). If you will confess, God has committed Himself in His faithfulness and His justice to forgive you and to cleanse you.

No matter what there might be on your conscience or in your heart right now, if you will confess that sin or those sins with faith in God's faithfulness, then it will be as if you had never committed a sin in your life. When God forgives our sins, He blots them out. He doesn't ever hold them against us again. *"I, even I, am He who blots out your transgressions for My own sake; and I will not remember your sins"* (Isaiah 43:25). Remember, you are not only forgiven, but you are also cleansed. There is nothing between you and God from this moment onward in that respect. Say out loud, "Thank You, God, for forgiving me. I receive Your forgiveness. Amen."

There is one more thing you may need to do. You may need to forgive yourself. Sometimes, that is the hardest part. Tell the Lord, "Because You have forgiven me, I forgive myself."

Unforgiveness toward Other People

The next barrier is closely related to the need to forgive yourself. It is an attitude of unforgiveness toward others. This attitude is also terribly common in the body of Christ. Jesus said,

> *And whenever you stand praying, if you have anything against anyone, forgive him, that your Father in heaven may also forgive you your trespasses.* (Mark 11:25)

Jesus was saying that when we are in the attitude of prayer, we should ask ourselves, before we start to pray, "Is there anyone I have something against?" He said this because if you pray with resentment and unforgiveness in your heart, these things will be barriers to the answer to your prayer. You want a clear communication channel with God and openness to receive what you pray for. Before you pray, therefore, forgive whatever is in your heart against anyone— and that leaves out no one. Then, you can pray.

You want a clear communication channel with God and openness to receive what you pray for.

Forgiveness is not an emotion but a decision—a decision of the will. I have explained to people that it is like having IOUs from somebody. To forgive is to tear up the IOUs. Once, while I was teaching, I addressed any wives in the meeting who might have been mistreated or abandoned by their husbands. I pointed out that even though they might have been treated very wrongly, they had to have an attitude of forgiveness toward their spouses. I told them, "You may have in your possession a handful of IOUs from your husband to you, which he has not fulfilled: 'I owe you love.' 'I owe you support.' 'I owe you care.' 'I owe you provision in many areas.' Those IOUs are absolutely legal, and you can hold on to them. But before you decide to do that, remember that God in heaven has in His hand many IOUs from you to Him. And He says, in so many words, 'Let's do a deal. You tear up your IOUs, and I'll tear up Mine. But if you hold on to yours, I'll hold on to Mine.'"

In the parable of the unmerciful servant, Jesus compared the proportion of what others owe us to what we owe God to somebody owing you the equivalent of about seventeen dollars, and you owing God the equivalent of six million dollars. (See Matthew 18:22–35.) From this perspective, it isn't super-spiritual to forgive people—it's enlightened self-interest! Anybody who won't let seventeen dollars go for the sake of being forgiven six million dollars doesn't have any business sense, to say the least!

In speaking to these wives and others who were at the meeting, I continued, "If you want God to tear up His IOUs from you, then you tear up your IOUs, whether they are from your husband, your parents, or someone else." When I finished my message, I didn't quite know what I was going to do next. Then, down the middle aisle came a very smartly dressed young lady who was about thirty years old. She was self-possessed and very sophisticated. This young woman marched right up to me and looked me full in the face. She was radiant as she said, "Mr. Prince, I just want to tell you that while you were preaching, I got rid of about thirty thousand dollars' worth of IOUs." Then, she turned around and walked out. She got the message. She didn't need counseling, and she didn't need prayer. She had done the right thing and was set free.

Let's take a few moments now to deal with resentment and unforgiveness in our hearts. Ask the Holy Spirit to show you if there is any hidden root of bitterness in you. The Bible says that if a root of bitterness springs up, it will defile many. (See Hebrews 12:15.) Then, you are going to make a decision to tear up those IOUs.

> **Ask the Holy Spirit to show you if there are areas of unforgiveness in your heart and life.**

If you are a young person, you may feel that your parents haven't treated you right. Unfortunately, that is very true in many circumstances today. But let me point out to you that the first commandment that carries a promise with it is *"Honor your father and mother"* (Ephesians 6:2). Again, it's a question of enlightened self-interest. You don't have to agree with everything they do, but you must have an attitude of respect toward them. I have never known a Christian who was truly blessed in God who had a wrong attitude toward his parents—never. It is an essential requirement for the blessing of God.

I'm not talking here about only a wrong attitude toward parents or husbands or wives, but those are some of the most common relationships in which unforgiveness can occur. Again, ask the Holy Spirit to show you if there are areas of unforgiveness in your heart and life:

Holy Spirit, I ask You now, in Jesus' name, to speak to my heart. Show me if there are areas of bitterness, resentment, and unforgiveness, and make me willing to forgive.

The Holy Spirit may give you a specific name or names or a specific situation. Now, pray this prayer:

Lord, if there has been any resentment, any unforgiveness, or any bitterness in my heart, I renounce it now. I lay it down. If anyone has ever harmed me or wronged me, I forgive them now as I would have You forgive me. I make the decision now to tear up all the IOUs I am presently holding. I forgive them in the name of Your Son Jesus, and I believe You forgive me. Thank You, Lord.

Involvement in the Occult

The next barrier, which is also very common today, is occult involvement—being in some way or having been involved in things like fortune-telling, Ouija
boards, horoscopes, or any of the innumerable ways
in which superstition and satanic cults have invaded
our contemporary culture. Invariably, these practices are barriers to healing. Many times, when Ruth
and I ministered, people came for healing, but there
was some dark shadow of the occult still over their
lives, and it came between them and the healing they
sought.

There are many forms of the occult. Much of contemporary music, hard rock and so on, is really satanic. It has demonic power in it. If we have exposed
ourselves to it, we could need deliverance from it. Another form of the occult is drug abuse. I won't give an
exhaustive list, but I am going to trust the Holy Spirit
to show you if this is a problem area for you.

Before we move on to renouncing the occult and to
praying for forgiveness, I want to relate a story as an
illustration. I was teaching in a certain place, and it
came time for Ruth and me to minister to the sick. A
young woman of about eighteen came up for prayer.
And as we looked in her eyes, we saw a glazed expression, which nearly always is the result of involvement
in the occult. We wanted to help deliver her before we
prayed for her healing, so I asked her, "Have you been

involved in the occult?" She said no. I felt she was being honest, but I wanted to probe. I said, "You haven't been to a fortune-teller, haven't played with a Ouija board?" No, none of those. "Have you had your horoscope read?" No. Still, there was this barrier. Then, God gave Ruth a word of knowledge: rock music. The girl went flat on her back without Ruth praying for her. That was the barrier. After that, she could be healed.

> **What wonderful promises. No sicknesses, and a guaranteed full life span. Who wouldn't want that?**

Our next step is to renounce every contact with the occult. In Exodus 23, Moses gave instructions to the children of Israel as to how they were to deal with the forms of worship and religion that had been in the land of Canaan before they arrived there. He warned them they were to have no part whatever in such satanic practices.

You shall not bow down to their gods, nor serve them, nor do according to their works; but you shall utterly overthrow them and completely break down their sacred pillars.

(Exodus 23:24)

In other words, there was to be no association with any of those kinds of occult practices. On the basis of that, Moses gave them these promises:

*So you shall serve the LORD your God, and He
will bless your bread and your water. And I
will take sickness away from the midst of you.
No one shall suffer miscarriage or be barren
in your land; I will fulfill the number of your
days.* (Exodus 24:25–26)

What wonderful promises. No barrenness, no miscarriages, no female problems, no sicknesses, and a guaranteed full life span. Who wouldn't want that? However, let us not detach these promises from the context. They are only for those who break totally with the occult in every form.

Years ago, I was in a typical charismatic house prayer meeting, and I found myself sitting next to a young man. I was just talking to him, and I asked, "Are you baptized in the Holy Spirit?" He replied, "Yes, but…." When anybody says "Yes, but…" to that question, it means, "But I don't speak in tongues."

I didn't discuss the matter with him, and I didn't have a specific plan. I just asked, "Did you ever go to a fortune-teller?" "Yes," he said, "once when I was a boy of about fifteen. But I just did it as a joke. I didn't believe it." I said, "You did go." He said, "Yes." So, I asked, "Would you be willing to acknowledge to God that that was a sin, and ask Him to forgive you and release you from its consequences?" I don't think he was impressed by my arguments. However, more or less just to get me off his back, he agreed. I led him in this simple prayer: "Lord, I confess that I went to a fortune-teller. I should not have done it. I realize it was a sin, and I ask You to forgive me and release me from its consequences, in Jesus' name." Then, I put my hand on him and prayed for him, and he spoke fluently in tongues. That was the invisible barrier.

Involvement in the occult is not just a barrier to the gifts of the Spirit, but it is also a barrier to healing. I would estimate that this barrier affects 50 percent of Christians. That number may be high, but the influence of the occult is so subtle today. There are so many different ways in which it is present in our society. You can go into a souvenir shop and unknowingly pick up some little idol and take it home as an ornament.

This is serious business. Some years ago, I ministered to a woman in Falls Church, Virginia, who was a judge on the supreme court of the State of Virginia. In a later chapter, I discuss how she was miraculously healed. After she was healed, a friend of hers won a free trip for two to Mexico in some competition. They went down to Mexico for a vacation, but when they came back, the friend phoned my wife and me in a desperate state. She said, "This lady has just tried to commit suicide. Come over and help us." We went over posthaste and started to talk to them. Apparently, nothing had changed. I said, "You've been down to Mexico?" They said yes. I asked, "Did you bring any souvenirs back with you?" The woman who was a judge said, "Yes, I brought one circular image." So, I said, "What was it an image of?" It was the sun god, and I explained, "That's your problem. You are under a curse because you have brought an accursed thing into your home. The Bible says that if you bring an accursed thing into your home, you are accursed just like the thing." (See Joshua 7.)

She was a woman of action. She got up, took the circular image down to the basement, broke it into small pieces, and put it in the trash can. That was the end of that; she never had another problem. But it nearly cost this woman her life. That is how real this is. God has an intense hatred of idolatry. I don't think we appreciate how much the Lord hates idolatry.

You now have an opportunity to renounce all occult involvement. If you have been involved in the occult, and you have dealt with it before God, then you are free. But if you have never dealt with it, allow the Holy Spirit to rest upon you right now and speak to you. He has a wonderful memory. He can take you back twenty years to something that happened in your past.

Pray the following prayer, but don't just read the words. Let it be your own acknowledgment before God.

Lord, if I've ever been involved in the occult, even in ignorance, whatever it was, I confess it as a sin, and I renounce it. I ask You to forgive me, and I make a commitment that I will never again knowingly be involved in the occult. Forgive me, Lord, and release me from its influence right now. I also ask You to guard me from this time on from the subtle influence of the occult, in all areas of my life, so that I do not unknowingly become involved in it. In the name of Jesus, amen.

Ungodly Covenants

Another barrier, which is related to the occult, is identified in the same chapter of Exodus:

You shall make no covenant with them, nor with their gods. (Exodus 23:32)

It is possible for people to enter into a covenant with other people who follow false gods. If you do that, you become involved in the guilt of those people and their false gods. This idea may seem remote and abstract to you, but I am going to give you an example of it. Some of you may be offended by it, but I say this in love because I know it to be true. A very common covenant group, a secret society that prevails throughout the English-speaking world, is Freemasonry. If you are involved in Freemasonry, you are under a curse—not only you, but also your family and your descendants. I speak from experience. Ruth and I have encountered this; we've dealt with it, and we've come to the root of it. Freemasonry is a false religious system. And whatever anyone may say, it is not a secret. The main ceremonies of Freemasonry are known and have been published by people who are not Freemasons.

To take only one aspect, the Royal Arch degree acknowledges a god whose name is Jabulon. *Ja* is short for Jehovah, *bul* is short for Baal, and *on* is short for Osiris— the Egyptian god of the underworld. Any system of worship that combines the true God with Baal and Osiris is abomination in the sight of the Lord. It makes no difference who practices it, even if it is the archbishop of Canterbury. God does not show favoritism.

> **Ruth and I laid hands on the young mother, and the power of God came on her.**

We have seen the most terrible consequences in people's lives and families because of this curse. I will give you one dramatic example. We held a healing service in Australia, and, one morning, one of the people who came forward was a young woman who had obviously been in the subculture but had apparently just come out of it. She had what appeared to be a newborn baby in her arms. We asked, "What do you need prayer for?" She said, "My baby." This baby looked about six days old, but the mother told us she was six weeks old. We asked what the problem was, and she said, "She just won't take any nourishment. I can't get her to take more than a spoonful of milk."

Ruth and I laid hands on the young mother as she was holding the baby in her arms, and the power of God came on her. She went down on the floor, and Ruth caught the baby out of her arms and held her. Then, God gave Ruth a word of knowledge. She said, "The girl's father is a Freemason." The people who were ministering to the young woman as she lay on the floor came against that spirit of Freemasonry, and it came out of her with a loud, prolonged shriek. But the dramatic thing was that exactly the same shriek came out of the baby in Ruth's arms at the same time!

Six hours later, the young mother came to the evening service with the little baby. She said, "I just want to tell you that between the morning and the evening, she's taken three full bottles!" Thank God for that. But that baby never would have been healed if the curse of Freemasonry had not first been broken.

If you are involved in Freemasonry, either directly or through your husband, father, or some other relative, you need to say a prayer of renunciation. There are also many other similar secret societies, cults, and satanic organizations in the world today. If you are involved in any of those groups, I ask you in the name of the Lord Jesus to renounce them now:

Lord Jesus Christ, I want to serve You and love You. If there is in my life, or in my family, a curse of Freemasonry or any other cult, I ask You to release me and forgive me and break its power over me right now, in Jesus' name. Amen.

The Effects of a Curse

The final barrier that I want to discuss is the effects of a curse. There are some common indications of a curse over a person's life or family. If several of these things apply to you or your family members, there is probably a curse over you. The good news is that Jesus was made a curse so that we might be redeemed from the curse and receive the blessing. (See Galatians 3:13–14.) Even so, most times, we need to specifically renounce the cause of the curse and claim the release.

The following are seven common indications of a curse:

1. A history of mental and emotional breakdown in your family.

2. Repeated and chronic sicknesses, especially hereditary ones, because the mark of a curse is that it passes from generation to generation.

3. Repeated miscarriages or female problems. As far as Ruth and I are concerned, when we pray for that kind of need, we automatically treat it as a curse. After ministry, we have seen many barren women able to conceive and bear children, and we have seen many women with female problems delivered. Tumors and other problems involving the female organs disappear when the curse is lifted.

4. The breakdown of marriages and family alienation. If your family has a history of marriages breaking up and different branches of the family being at war with one another, you can almost be sure there is a curse.

5. Continuing financial insufficiency; never getting out of the poverty syndrome.

6. Being accident-prone. You are one of those people whom accidents just look for. You step off the curb, and you break your ankle. You close the car door on your fingers. I have observed with such people that just when they are getting near to the point of deliverance, they are tripped up. It's just amazing. In deliverance services I've held in the past, people have wanted to drive as many as 100 miles to come, but the car broke down on the way, and they never got there. Why? It was a curse.

7. A history of suicides or unnatural deaths.

If you are under a curse, may it be lifted from you as you pray. You can become a different person. A curse is like a dark shadow that always seems to hover over you. Or, it's like a hand that reaches out from the past. Every time you are about to succeed, it trips you up. If I had to choose one key word to describe the effects of a curse, it would be *frustration*. I have dealt with many people who had all the qualifications for success, yet time and time again they were on the verge of success when something went wrong. It was the effect of a curse.

> *A curse is like a dark shadow that hovers over you, but you can become a different person.*

The Holy Spirit is able to deal with any kind of curse in your life. Take a moment to reflect on your life. Look back over it. Consider if it has the marks that I have described. Then, say this prayer:

Thank You, Lord Jesus, that on the cross You were made a curse so that I might be redeemed from the curse and enter into the blessing. Because of what You did, I release myself from every curse over me and my family, in Your precious name, and I claim the blessing that You purchased for me with Your blood. Thank You, Lord Jesus.

SOME SICKNESSES ARE CAUSED BY EVIL SPIRITS

There is one other fact you need to be aware of. Sometimes, sicknesses are caused by, or associated with, the presence of evil spirits, as we saw earlier in the example of the young mother with her baby. Frequently, the ministry of healing also includes the ministry of driving out evil spirits. This isn't done in some churches, but Jesus cast out evil spirits when He was on earth, and He still does. Let's look at a biblical example of this.

> *When the sun was setting, all those who had any that were sick with various diseases brought them to [Jesus]; and He laid His hands on every one of them and healed them. And demons [evil spirits] also came out of many, crying out.*
> (Luke 4:40–41)

Notice that associated with the ministry of the laying on of hands for healing was the driving out of demons. When the supernatural power of God comes into operation, evil spirits just can't stand it any longer; they have to come out.

Direct Association

There are two main ways in which evil spirits are associated with sickness. The first is that they are the direct causes of sickness. These are spirits of infirmity, of pain, of crippling, and of death, to name only four that we deal with commonly. For instance, curvature or deformity of the spine is frequently caused by a crippling spirit. For a person who has this malady to receive full release, it is necessary to drive out that crippling spirit.

Jesus encountered a woman who was bent over double and couldn't stand up straight. He did not treat her problem as a physical sickness. Instead, He said she had been bound by a spirit of infirmity for eighteen years. He loosed her from the spirit, and, immediately, she straightened up. (See Luke 13:10–16.)

I have dealt with all four of the evil spirits mentioned above many times. The spirit of death is very common. It causes a person to be infirm and weak, and ultimately to die prematurely. Such a person often has a morbid outlook on life. He or she will tend to look on the dark side of things and may be inclined to wear dark clothing. There's something morose about him or her. I have had to say to several young ladies, "I suggest you don't wear black any longer." You may think this advice is strange, and I'm not saying that people should never wear black. However, there are just some people for whom it isn't altogether wise to wear black because of its association.

Ruth and I probably dealt with hundreds of cases of people who needed deliverance from the spirit of death. As always, we discovered the right thing to do was to replace the negative with the positive. One way the spirit of death is enabled to enter in is when people become discouraged, disheartened, and oppressed, and they say, "I might as well be dead. I wish I were dead. What's the good of living?" When you say that, it's an invitation to the spirit of death to come in and take over. And that spirit doesn't need many invitations. One of the most dangerous things a person can ever say is, "I wish I were dead."

"Emotional Spirits"

The second main way in which evil spirits are associated with sickness is through what I call "emotional spirits." These do not directly cause sickness, but they cause an attitude in you that makes you incapable of receiving your healing. The commonest is rejection, which is the sense that "Nobody really loves me," "I was never wanted," "My parents didn't care for me," "My husband deserted me," or "When I walk into a room, everyone stops talking." That sort of thing. I would say that about 50 percent of people in America today have a problem with rejection because parents have failed their children, husbands have failed their wives, and wives have failed their husbands. They need emotional healing. And sometimes, when a person comes for physical healing, God is more interested in the emotional healing than the physical.

In addition, a spirit of grief is common. It usually comes out of some personal tragedy. There is also a spirit of depression—but no Christian would know anything about that, would he? And there is also a spirit of tension. Many times, when people have back pain, it is caused by a spirit of tension. When they are released from the tension, the pain tends to go. There are many other emotional spirits, but these will give you an idea of them.

You have an opportunity now to revoke the negative things you have been saying about yourself. In Psalm 118:17, the psalmist says,

> **Revoke the negative things you have been saying about yourself, and affirm, "I'm not going to let the devil trample over my emotions and my attitudes."**

I shall not die, but live, and declare the works of the LORD.

That is a positive decision. Repeat it until you are full of positive faith. I suggest that you stand up and say it, because there is something about being in a standing position that helps you to affirm, "I'm not going to lie down under the devil. I'm not going to let him trample over my emotions and my attitudes." You may even want to make this declaration to another believer.

After you have spoken the declaration, say, "Praise You, Lord Jesus. Thank You, Lord Jesus. Glory to Your name. Victory through the blood of the Lamb and through the name of Jesus. Amen and amen."

SEEK HEALING

Now that we have identified and worked through the invisible barriers to healing, you can seek healing from the Lord. Jesus said, *"These signs will follow those who believe: In My name they will...lay hands on the sick, and they will recover"* (Mark 16:17–18). This Scripture doesn't say that all of them will be instantly healed. Again, sometimes healing is instantaneous, and sometimes it's progressive. But regardless, healing comes.

When I met Ruth, she was flat on her back—virtually an invalid. I laid hands on her, prayed for her, and said, "Now, keep the plug in. Stay with your plug into God's power outlet." I told her the way to keep the plug in was to keep thanking Him until the healing was completed. That was in June. She kept the plug in until November, and by November her healing was completed. She'd had a ruptured disc in her spine, and her spine had been curved since childhood. Now she has no ruptured disc, and she has a straight spine. But she did not get an instant miracle. She got a progressive work.

You may be instantaneously healed, or you may receive a healing that begins. If it begins, keep your plug in. If you say, "I didn't get healed; nothing happened," do you know what you have done? You have pulled the plug out. If you say, "God touched me, and I'm going to keep thanking Him until it's complete," it will be complete.

Finally, periodically examine your life in light of the invisible barriers to healing we have discussed in this chapter, particularly in regard to unbelief, unconfessed sin, and unforgiveness, in order to stay in right relationships with God and man and to remain open for your healing.

Chapter Ten

The Helmet of Hope: Freedom from Depression

Many people's wholeness in Christ is hindered by depression. No matter what degree of depression they suffer from, it has an effect on their peace of mind, their relationships with others, their productiveness—and, significantly, their spiritual growth. It prevents them from experiencing the abundant life Christ desires to give them. In this chapter, I want to discuss, on the basis of personal experience, how depression is often a spiritual problem that needs to be dealt with by prayer, deliverance, and the Word of God.

OUR SPIRITUAL PROTECTION

In Ephesians 6, Paul wrote about our spiritual warfare and our spiritual armor.

Finally, my brethren, be strong in the Lord and in the power of His might. Put on the whole armor of God, that you may be able to stand against the wiles of the devil. For we do not wrestle against flesh and blood, but against principalities, against powers, against the rulers of the darkness of this age, against spiritual hosts of wickedness in the heavenly places. Therefore take up the whole armor of God, that you may be able to withstand in the evil day, and having done all, to stand. Stand therefore, having girded your waist with truth, having put on the breastplate of righteousness, and having shod your feet with the preparation of the gospel of peace; above all, taking the shield of faith with which you will be able to quench all the fiery darts of the wicked one. And take the helmet of salvation, and the sword of the Spirit, which is the word of God; praying always with all prayer and supplication in the Spirit, being watchful to this end with all perseverance and supplication for all the saints.

(Ephesians 6:10–18)

This passage is one of many in the New Testament that show clearly that as believers in Jesus Christ, we are involved in a tremendous spiritual conflict. It also tells us that God the Father has made provision for our protection through spiritual armor. The helmet of "the hope of salvation" (see also 1 Thessalonians 5:8) is one particular aspect of the spiritual protection God has made available to us, which I learned to use because of my own need. This helmet of hope leads to renewal of the mind and is an essential part of our spiritual covering as Christians, particularly in regard to depression.

A STRUGGLE AGAINST DEPRESSION

The helmet of hope leads to renewal of the mind.

Let me relate to you how I became aware of my need in this area. The Lord graciously saved me and baptized me in the Holy Spirit in 1941 and called me into His service. In 1946, I stepped out into full-time ministry. From 1949 onward, for about nine years, I was pastor of a congregation in London, England. During that period, I had a certain measure of success in my ministry. We regularly saw people saved, healed, and baptized in the Holy Spirit. In those days, that was not something that was happening everywhere, by any means. Those were very dry, barren days—especially, I believe, in England. So, there was a real measure of fruit and result from our ministry.

Even so, I had various personal problems for which I did not have any answer. In particular, I had a problem of recurrent fits of depression that would come over me like a kind of dark, heavy cloud and seem to press me down, close me in, and shut me off from normal communication with other people, even my family. The embarrassing thing to me was that it seemed that when I went around with this cloud hanging over me, I projected this pressure onto the people whom I was with. And again, I was particularly conscious of the effect on my own family.

I struggled against this depression by every means in my power that I knew of. I prayed, I fasted, I made resolutions, I got up early, I stayed up late—I did everything that I knew to do, but it got no better. In fact, the more I prayed and fasted, the worse it became! That was very discouraging. I remember one of our daughters, who was about fifteen years old at the time, saying to me one day, "Daddy, please don't fast. You're worse when you fast." Of course, that isn't the way to encourage a preacher. Yet it was true because fasting brought the thing out into the open, but it didn't resolve the problem.

A REVELATION OF "THE SPIRIT OF HEAVINESS"

I had come to the end of my solutions, and, one day—I was actually fasting at the time, which I mention as a little indication that fasting does not go unrewarded—I was reading the Bible, and I read this phrase in Isaiah 61:3:

The garment of praise for the spirit of heaviness.

When I read that phrase, *"the spirit of heaviness,"* I suddenly realized by revelation of the Holy Spirit that this was my problem. I was dealing with an evil spirit, a personality who studied me, followed me around, knew my weaknesses, and knew how and when to attack me. I was not dealing merely with some mental or psychological conditions in myself. I was not dealing merely with some habit pattern. There was a being, set against me by Satan himself, who was studying me and plotting my downfall.

I saw then why the pressure became worse the more I wanted to serve the Lord. This evil spirit had been commissioned to hinder me in my service for God. When I was somewhat slack and indifferent, the pressure was lifted. But the more dedicated and earnest I became, the worse the pressure became. Again, looking at it in that way, I saw clear indications that I was dealing with a personality with understanding who knew just how and when to apply the pressure. I also saw that this was something that ran in my family. I realized that, for many years, my father had experienced the same type of pressure from time to time.

I often deal with people who have prolonged, serious depression. More and more, I am coming to the conclusion that in almost every case, it is connected with involvement in the occult. Before I was a Christian, I had been involved in the occult quite extensively, particularly in the field of yoga. It was not until many years later that I saw the connection between my involvement in yoga and the spirit of depression.

Wherever I deal with a person who has prolonged, serious fits of depression, I am almost convinced that somewhere he has trespassed into Satan's territory in the realm of the occult. Many times, he will deny it, sometimes indignantly. But when I work with him and bring the truth out, it nearly always turns out that way.

A PROMISE OF DELIVERANCE

At last, I had come to realize the identity of my enemy. This was a tremendous advance. I would say that when I recognized what I was dealing with and specifically that it was a spirit being, I was 80 percent of the way to victory. I needed only one other Scripture to bring me the solution to my problem:

> *It shall come to pass, that **whosoever** shall call on the name of the LORD shall be delivered.*
> (Joel 2:32 KJV, emphasis added)

175

I saw that this promise, in its own way, was just as all-inclusive as John 3:16: *"God so loved the world, that he gave his only begotten Son, that **whosoever** believeth in him* [shall] *not perish, but have everlasting life"* (KJV, emphasis added).

> *I claimed God's own promise:* **"Whosoever shall call on the name of the LORD shall be delivered."**

I also recognized that Joel 2:32 was distinctively a promise of deliverance. I put together Isaiah 61:3 and Joel 2:32, and I prayed specifically to God the Father in Jesus' name.

I want to emphasize the importance of praying specifically. I named the evil spirit, "the spirit of heaviness," and I claimed God's own promise: *"Whosoever shall call on the name of the LORD shall be delivered."*

I did not understand the deliverance ministry in any sense in which I understand it now, but I was driven by personal need to put these two Scriptures together. I prayed, "God, in the name of the Lord Jesus Christ, according to Your Word, I'm asking You to deliver me from this spirit of heaviness." And when I prayed that specific, scriptural prayer, I was delivered. The pressure was lifted. Praise God for deliverance!

THE BATTLE FOR THE MIND

But then, I learned by experience that it is one thing to *be* delivered, and it is another thing to *stay* delivered. God began to show me that He had done His part of the job, and now I had to do my part. He had set my mind free from this demonic pressure. Now, it was up to me to reeducate my mind, to cultivate a totally different kind of outlook and way of thinking. Before I was delivered, I was not able to do it. After I was delivered, it was my responsibility to do it.

I believe this process is true in almost any realm in which God intervenes on our behalf, whether it is salvation, healing, or deliverance. God does His part, and then it's up to us to do our part. Our part is to maintain, to persevere, to hold on to what God has given us.

In fighting this battle to preserve my deliverance from depression, I became aware that the main problem area in my life was that of my mind. The devil was continually reaching me through my mind. I happen to have had the privilege of a very elaborate, prolonged, and sophisticated intellectual education. I had intricate training in the realm of analytical thinking. In this regard, I discovered that the more highly refined and cultivated a person's mind is, the more vulnerable it is to Satan. The more you trust in your mind, the more you have learned to lean upon it, the more Satan is able to use it against you. I realized that I had to fight this battle for the control of my own mind.

I don't think there are many Christians who really do control their own minds. I remember the testimony of a woman who said God showed her that she must teach her mind and her thoughts that they were the servant, not the master.

> *Our thoughts should not be our masters; they should be our servants.*

There are many areas in our lives that we have to bring into subjection to the spiritual element within us. Another one, frankly, is the stomach. The stomach has good and necessary purposes, but it is not to be the master; it is to be the servant. My good friend Don Basham said that he came to the place where he told his stomach, "You don't tell me when to eat. I tell you." That is establishing control over a major area of your life.

The same is true in our thought life. Our thoughts should not be our masters; they should be our servants. Again, I believe there are comparatively few Christians who really have control in the realm of their own thought lives. They are carried to and fro, they are tossed up and down, they are subject to all sorts of pressures that, in many cases, they cannot adequately handle because they have treated their thoughts as their masters rather than their servants.

PROTECTION FOR THE MIND

I came to see that what I needed above all else was protection for my mind. Then, it occurred to me that there was a passage in Ephesians 6, which I included at the beginning of this chapter, about God the Father's provision of protection. Reading about just the armor, which is listed in verses 14 through 17, you will see that there are six items of equipment—the first five are used for defensive purposes and the sixth for offensive ones.

1. The belt of truth. (verse 14)

2. The breastplate of righteousness. (verse 14)

3. The shoes or boots of the preparation of the gospel of peace. (verse 15)

4. The shield of faith. (verse 16)

5. The helmet of salvation. (verse 17)

6. The sword of the Spirit. (verse 17)

These items of equipment are made effective through the weapon that Charles Wesley, in one of his hymns, called "the weapon of all prayer"—*"praying*

always with all prayer and supplication in the Spirit"
(Ephesians 6:18). So, actually, the complete list is sev-
enfold. In Ephesians 6, there are six items of defensive and offensive equipment, plus the weapon of "all
prayer."

As I studied this list, I realized that if a believer
puts on each piece of equipment, he is completely pro-
tected from the crown of his head to the soles of his
feet—on one condition. What is the condition? That
he doesn't turn his back, because there is no protection for the back. If you say, "It's no good; I can't do it
anymore; I'm giving up," that's turning a defenseless
back to the devil. And, believe me, he'll pour his fiery
darts in and wound you in various ways. We have to
stay facing the enemy.

It also occurred to me that there was one piece
of equipment that was obviously designed to protect
the mind: the helmet of salvation. The helmet covers
the head, which is associated with the thought life. I
saw that God had provided me with protection for my
mind.

THE PLACE OF HOPE IN A BELIEVER'S LIFE

Then, I said to myself, *I know I'm saved; I have
salvation. Does that mean that I automatically have*

the helmet, or is there more to it than that? Fortunately, I had a Bible that included cross references. The cross reference to Ephesians 6:17, "the helmet," was 1 Thessalonians 5:8. I turned to that verse and read,

> *But let us who are of the day be sober, putting on the breastplate of faith and love, and as a helmet the hope of salvation.*

There I saw that the helmet is specified—it is called *"the hope of salvation."* Suddenly, the Holy Spirit quickened for me one word out of this Scripture: *hope.* I realized how little thought or study I had given to the place of hope in the life of the believer. The Holy Spirit led me from Scripture to Scripture through the New Testament, showing me that my whole spiritual experience was unbalanced and incomplete without a proper understanding of the place of hope as the protection of my mind.

Understanding the place of hope as the protection of your mind will bring balance to your spiritual life.

I want to give you just some of the Scriptures to which the Holy Spirit led me. We'll begin with the last verse of 1 Corinthians 13, that famous chapter on love. Paul said,

Now abide faith, hope, love, these three.

(verse 13)

In the context of the chapter, it is clear that these are the three continuing realities of spiritual experience in the Christian life. Other things, Paul said, are temporary. They have a purpose, and when their purpose is fulfilled, they will no longer be needed. But the abiding three realities of spiritual experience are faith, hope, and love.

I had heard many sermons on faith, and many sermons on love, but I had never once heard a sermon on hope. I had to preach myself my first sermon on hope.

FAITH IS IN THE HEART, AND HOPE IS IN THE MIND

Let's return to a theme we discussed in chapter three—the distinct meanings in Scripture given to faith and hope—because the differences are important to our understanding of the helmet of hope. Faith and hope are located in different areas of the human personality.

We have seen that biblical faith is in the realm of the heart. First Thessalonians 5:8 refers to *"the breastplate of faith and love."* The breast is the area

182

of the heart, so faith and love are in the heart. Then, Romans 10:10 says, *"With the heart one believes unto righteousness."* All through the New Testament, faith is not depicted as being in the realm of the mind but in the realm of the heart.

When you really believe something in your heart, you can't help believing it. You don't have to argue about it or prove it to anybody. To repeat an earlier example, I believe my sins are forgiven. I believe it in my heart. No matter who might argue with me about it, it wouldn't change my belief in the least. I don't need to argue about what I really believe. Yet, if I were trying to prove to myself that a particular miracle would take place, I think it is very unlikely that the miracle would occur unless that knowledge were in my heart, as well.

From the Head to the Heart

God has given me a certain measure of faith for miracles. At times, when I am ministering, people come up to me with unbelief, but I can tell them the miracle will happen because I have faith at that time that it will occur. There is an absolute quiet assurance that is heart faith. Many times, God's Word has reached our heads—we have knowledge of the truth—but it hasn't reached our hearts. It often takes longer for God's Word to get into our hearts than it does to get into our heads.

Almost every major biblical truth that I believe today I have preached myself into believing. I started preaching it because I saw it in the Bible and thought, *If it's in the Bible, it's true. I'll declare it.* Then, one day, I woke up to the pleasant realization that I really had it. I had preached myself into believing it with my heart.

Furthermore, the Scripture says it's legitimate to say something with your mouth in order to get it to your heart. But we must be very sincere and not pretend it's in our hearts before it's really there. In that famous passage of Romans 10:8–10, Paul put the heart and the mouth together three times. The first two times, it is the mouth first, and then the heart. The last time, it is the heart first, and then the mouth.

> **God's promises work when you not only confess with your mouth but also believe in your heart.**

This truth was brought home to me by the fact that in the Hebrew language, to learn a thing by heart is to learn it by the mouth. In other words, you learn something by heart by saying it over and over again until it's no effort to repeat it.

If you understand what you're doing spiritually, it is legitimate to confess yourself into heart faith using the Word of God, the Bible. *"So then faith comes by hearing, and hearing by the word of God"* (Romans

10:17). But don't forget that God's promises don't work until you not only confess with your mouth but also believe in your heart. I have met many people who were busy confessing the Word with their mouths who didn't yet have it in their hearts.

Mental Faith

Not once can I recall a person who argued that he had faith receive what he said he had faith for. The Bible says that boasting is excluded. By what law? The law of faith. (See Romans 3:27.) So, if you really have faith, you should not boast about it. Much of our arguing is not really trying to prove it to others; it's trying to prove it to ourselves. And if we have to prove it to ourselves, we don't have it. Many times, I've heard Christians say, "I know I have faith," but what they have is just knowledge.

I'm not saying this to be critical or unkind, but it has resolved a great problem for me: Why do many people say they have faith but don't get what they say they have faith for? Because they have knowledge of the Word in their minds but not in their hearts. In my experience, so many times, the person who thinks he has faith gets nothing, while the person who says, "I don't think I have faith" receives what he is seeking. This is because the person who doesn't have much knowledge may have heart faith, and it is heart faith that produces results. It is often very hard to know what is in your own heart. Jeremiah 17:9 says, *"The heart is deceitful above all things, and desperately wicked; who can know it?"* At times, we may not recognize when we have sinned, but at other times, we may not recognize when we have developed heart faith.

HOPE IS PROTECTION FOR THE MIND

With that perspective, let's focus on hope. The difference between faith and hope is that faith is in the heart, while hope is in the mind. Another difference is that faith is something that you have right now, and hope is directed toward the future. Faith is belief or conviction of truth, while hope is confident expectation. It is legitimate to have hope in your mind for the future, but it is incorrect to talk about faith in your mind for the future. That isn't faith.

The protection of the believer's mind—against depression, fear, and all sorts of negative thoughts—is the helmet of the hope of salvation. I believe every Christian, logically, must be an optimist. For a Christian to be a pessimist is, in effect, a denial of his faith.

If you want a basis in Scripture for the fact that every believer should be an optimist, there are many such verses, but I think Romans 8:28 is sufficient here:

We know that all things work together for good to those who love God, to those who are the called according to His purpose.

If you love God, and if you are sincerely seeking to walk in His purposes—note that it is not unconditional—then all things work together for good to you. And, if all things are working together for good to you, there can be no reason for pessimism. Every situation is a situation for optimism.

WHAT IS HOPE?

One's general outlook on life is often an inborn tendency, which we need to learn to place under the control of the Holy Spirit. There are generally two kinds of people born into the world—the pessimist and the optimist. A common way of defining the difference between them is that if they both walk into a room and see a glass filled halfway with water, the optimist says the glass is half full, and the pessimist says the glass is half empty. Both are looking at the same glass. It's an attitude of mind.

I was undoubtedly born a pessimist. Furthermore, I was brought up to be a pessimist—I was systematically trained that way. In my family, it was essentially a sin to be an optimist. If you weren't worrying, then you ought to be worrying about the fact that you weren't worrying. That may sound comical, but it was basically true. I meet many other people like that. They feel guilty if they're not anxious.

When the Holy Spirit led me to Isaiah 61:3 and Joel 2:32, God showed me that He had set my mind free from the oppression of the spirit of heaviness. My mind, which had been captivated, was now liberated. But, as I mentioned, I needed to learn to maintain my freedom through retraining my mind and thoughts. God was not going to retrain it for me. It was my responsibility. I began that retraining through learning the nature of hope.

> **Hope can be defined as "a confident, mental expectation of good."**

Hope can be defined as "a confident, mental expectation of good." We must learn to cultivate a totally different outlook on our lives, with different mental patterns and reactions. We have to learn positive, hope-filled attitudes, such as we find in Romans 8:28. We must discipline our minds by applying them to this retraining.

To battle depression or other negative thoughts in your own life, it is your responsibility to take action in the light of the Word of God. Scripture says,

For the weapons of our warfare are not carnal but mighty in God for pulling down strongholds, casting down arguments and every high thing that exalts itself against the knowledge of God, bringing every thought into captivity to the obedience of Christ. (2 Corinthians 10:4–5)

It is our responsibility to bring our thoughts into captivity to the obedience of Christ. This means obedience to God's Word. We have an obligation to think about every situation, every person, every problem as the Word of God speaks about them. We have to train ourselves to do this over time; it does not happen overnight.

It has been many years since this crisis came into my life, and I praise God that I still have mental victory. I have control over my own thoughts. I know I'm not perfect, but I also know there has been a total revolution. It began with deliverance, but it was completed by self-discipline in the area of the thoughts.

Of course, if you are not first delivered from the spirits that bind and oppress you—depression, fear, loneliness, suicide, self-pity, misery, torment, and many others—then for me to tell you to cultivate new thought patterns is like a drill sergeant giving orders to a group of soldiers whose feet are chained together. They can hear the orders, but their feet can't move to carry out the orders. Yet, while deliverance is an essential part of God's provision, it's not the whole of it. First deliverance, then retraining—retraining your appetites, retraining your emotions, and retraining your actions.

Before I continue describing how hope protects our minds, therefore, let's take a moment to pray for deliverance from any depression, fear, or related problems you may have that are connected with the mind.

Lord, I have come to understand the identity of my enemy—it is not just thoughts of depression, fear, self-pity, torment, or suicide, but it is an evil spirit that seeks to undermine and destroy my life. Through Christ, I have exchanged the spirit of heaviness for the garment of praise. You have said that whoever calls on the name of the Lord will be delivered. In the name of the Lord Jesus Christ, according to Your Word, I ask You to deliver me from this evil spirit and all the ways in which it manifests itself in my life. Thank You for Your complete deliverance from what has bound me. From this moment, help me to renew my mind daily in accordance with Your Word and will.

If you have prayed this prayer, give praise and thanks to God for His complete deliverance.

FAITH PRODUCES HOPE

In unfolding the nature of hope, we have closely examined the differences between faith (believing) and hope. Now, let's look at the interrelationship between these two spiritual realities. As I understand it, faith is the foundation, and hope is the product. Romans 4:18 describes how Abraham received the promise of God concerning the birth of his son Isaac long after it was physically possible for either him or his wife to have a child.

> *[For Abraham, human reason for] hope being gone, hoped in faith that he should become the father of many nations, as he had been promised.* (AMP)

Abraham believed, and, as a result, he hoped. Believing came first, and hoping was the product, or outcome, of his belief. I think this concept is expressed even more clearly in Hebrews 11:1:

> *Now faith is the substance of things hoped for, the evidence of things not seen.*

Faith is the underlying bedrock of assurance on which hope is supported. Faith, therefore, produces hope. To have hope without faith may be self-deception, but when you have faith, then you are entitled to hope. *"Faith is the substance of things hoped for."* Again, faith is in the heart, while hope is in the

> **Faith is the underlying bedrock of assurance on which hope is supported.**

mind. Faith is in the now, while hope is for the future. Both are legitimate, but we must have them in the right place and in the right relationship.

Let's look next at what the Bible says about the importance of hope in this context. Hope is one of the most beautiful themes in the Bible. The Holy Spirit opened up a completely new field of understanding to me regarding this truth. Before I had the crisis with depression, I had never seen that hope is essential. You just cannot get by without hope. You must have hope! Romans 8:24 says,

For we were saved in this hope.

We can put this the other way around, as well—no hope, no salvation. When you lose your hope, then, experientially, you have lost your salvation. When you are not living in hope, you are no longer living in the benefits of salvation. I don't mean you've lost salvation but that your experience of salvation has gone. We are saved in hope.

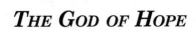

THE GOD OF HOPE

Romans 15:13 is another wonderful verse on hope. Let's look at the first part:

Now may the God of hope....

Did you know that the Lord is the God of hope? He is not merely the God of peace, the God of joy, the God of righteousness, and the God of power, but He is also the God of hope. The entire verse says,

Now may the God of hope fill you with all joy and peace in believing, that you may abound in hope by the power of the Holy Spirit.

When you are filled with faith through believing, this is the result: you abound in hope. You have hope bubbling up and overflowing within you. This hope is produced by the power of the Holy Spirit. One of the scriptural evidences of the Holy Spirit at work in a believer is abounding hope. Where hope ceases to abound, that person is no longer filled with the Holy Spirit; He has "leaked out."

> **When you are filled with faith through believing, you abound in hope.**

Ephesians 2:12 is a somber picture of the lost, those who do not know God:

At that time you were without Christ, being aliens from the commonwealth of Israel and strangers from the covenants of promise, having no hope and without God in the world.

This verse says that the lost are without three things: without Christ, without hope, and without God the Father. When you are without hope, you are without Christ and without God the Father. Hope is that important.

CHRIST IN YOU, THE HOPE OF GLORY

Let's look at a corresponding Scripture on the positive side.

The mystery [of the gospel]*...has been hidden from ages and from generations, but now has been revealed to His saints* [believers]. *To them God willed to make known what are the riches of the glory of this mystery among the Gentiles: which is....* (Colossians 1:26–27)

The whole gospel centers on this great and wonderful revelation that was kept secret from all the prophets and sages and great men of past generations but is now revealed to believers like you and me. What is this tremendous revelation?

...Christ in you, the hope of glory. (verse 27)

If we have no hope of eternal glory, we don't have Christ in us, because Christ in us is the hope of eternal glory. Our salvation depends on hope. When we're lost, we're without Christ, and we're without hope. But when we have Christ in us, we have the hope of glory—hope for the future and eternal life.

Paul said, *"If in this life only we have hope in Christ, we are of all men the most pitiable"*

(1 Corinthians 15:19). There is a future. The one who has Christ in him has hope for that future—a glorious, radiant, confident expectation of eternal glory with almighty God, the holy angels, and the redeemed of all ages—from age to age to age. That is what you have when you have Christ in you. If you are becoming uncertain or insecure about that hope, you had better check on your spiritual condition, because it is questionable whether you really have Christ in you. Christ in you is the hope of glory.

> **The one who has Christ in him has hope for eternal glory with almighty God and the redeemed of all ages.**

HOPE IS A REFUGE AND ANCHOR

Next, we turn to two of the most beautiful pictures in all Scripture. The writer of Hebrews was emphasizing the tremendous basis we have for our faith in Christ, and he wrote,

That by two immutable things [things incapable of change], *in which it is impossible for God to lie....*   (Hebrews 6:18)

What are the two unchangeable things? Verse 17 tells us that they are (1) God's *"counsel"* or Word,

195

and (2) God's *"oath."* God did not only speak something, but He also confirmed it with an oath. The Scriptures say that because there was nothing greater by which God could swear, He swore by Himself. (See verse 13.)

> *By myself have I sworn, saith the LORD* [to Abraham], *for because thou hast done this thing, and hast not withheld thy son, thine only son: that in blessing I will bless thee, and in multiplying I will multiply thy seed as the stars of the heaven, and as the sand which is upon the sea shore.* (Genesis 22:16–17 KJV)

The writer of Hebrews underscored the blessing given to Abraham by including the word *"innumerable"*:

> *Therefore from one man, and him as good as dead, were born as many as the stars of the sky in multitude; innumerable as the sand which is by the seashore.* (Hebrews 11:12)

We have two unchangeable things, in which it is impossible for God to lie, upon which to base our faith. In light of this,

> *...we might have strong consolation, who have fled for refuge to lay hold of the hope set before us.* (Hebrews 6:18)

That's the first picture of hope—a refuge. Then he moves on to a second picture:

This hope we have as an anchor of the soul, both sure and steadfast, and which enters the Presence behind the veil, where the forerunner has entered for us, even Jesus, having become High Priest forever according to the order of Melchizedek. (Hebrews 6:19–20)

Our Refuge

The writer of Hebrews used these two pictures in swift succession to show what the hope of salvation will do for the believer in his spiritual experience. First, he said, "We have fled to this hope for a refuge." I believe this imagery is taken from the Old Testament where, if an innocent man was being pursued by the avengers of blood and wanted a place of refuge from which the avengers would not dare to snatch him away, he fled to the tabernacle or the temple and took hold of the horns of the altar. As long as that innocent man held on to the horns of the altar, nobody dared to pull him away. That was his place of refuge. (See Exodus 21:12–14; 1 Kings 1:50–53; 2:28–32.)

All the forces of hell can never overcome us as long as we hold on to our hope in Jesus Christ.

When we come to the spiritual altar—which is the sacrifice of Christ—even if all the forces of hell seek to drag us away, as long as we hold on to the horns of that altar, we cannot be torn away.

What is the analogy for "the horns of the altar"? Our hope in Jesus Christ. Again, the sacrifice of Christ is the altar, and the horns—or the strength—of the altar is our hope. We have this hope as a refuge that we can flee to. So, when all the forces of hell are turned loose against you and are pressuring you from every side, and you don't seem to know where you can go to find an escape, flee to the altar and take hold of the horns, our hope in Jesus Christ.

The first picture, therefore, is of a person under tremendous, urgent, spiritual pressure, who is looking for a place of absolute security. He takes hold of "the horns of the altar"—the finished work of Christ and the hope of eternal glory.

Our Anchor

The second picture is perhaps even more beautiful. It is *"an anchor of the soul, both sure and steadfast"* that passes out of time into eternity and enters behind the veil, fastening to the great Rock of Ages, Jesus Christ, our High Priest and our Forerunner.

When I was going through my own struggle with depression, God the Father, through the Holy Spirit, began to deal with me about the spiritual truth in this picture of an anchor. His teaching went something like this. He asked, "What needs an anchor?" I said, "Lord, a ship or a boat needs an anchor." He said, "Why does the ship or the boat need an anchor?" I said, "Lord, because essentially a ship or a boat floats in an unstable, impermanent element of water."

The ship is made for the water, and it belongs in it, but there is nothing in that water that the ship can lay hold of for permanent security. So, it needs an anchor, which travels from the boat, through the unstable element of water, and onto the stable element of rock or earth below. When the anchor has passed from the boat, through the water, and onto the rock, the boat is stabilized and made secure.

Hebrews says our hope in Christ is the anchor for our souls. We are living in a very impermanent, unstable world. No matter how much financial and material security you may have—no matter how much insurance you may have, no matter how much money you may have in the bank, and no matter what other steps you may have taken for your security (and I'm not criticizing any of them)—the truth of the matter is, none of them really grants you security. Not one. They are like the water that the ship is in.

There is nothing that exists in time that is permanent, that is secure, that we can take hold of.

Everything we see is moving, it's flowing. It's here, but then, it passes away. The Scriptures say, *"All flesh is* [as] *grass, and all its loveliness is like the flower of the field. The grass withers, the flower fades"* (Isaiah 40:6–7). Grass or flowers may spring up in the morning, but, by the evening, they may be cut down and withered. That's what human life is like from an eternal perspective. It's very important that we never lose sight of that fact.

When my father died, he had an Anglican funeral in Great Britain. The Anglican prayer book has a beautiful burial service. It includes a number of Scriptures, and one of them is, *"Man who is born of woman is of few days and full of trouble. He comes forth like a flower and fades away"* (Job 14:1–2). As I sat at my father's funeral listening to those words, I said to myself, *That's the truth.* You can argue about it, and you can do your best to hide from it, but the fact is that *"man who is born of woman is of few days and full of trouble."*

When you are in Christ, you have a right to cast your anchor onto the "Rock of Ages."

There is therefore no place of security in this world. You have to move your anchor through the water and onto the Rock before you can be secure. The water represents this world, and the rock represents Christ. When you are in Christ, you have a right to cast your anchor onto the "Rock of Ages," and all the storms, tempests, and hurricanes that blow will never detach you from that Rock. The way we anchor onto that Rock is by hope. Our hope is assured by the two immutable things by which God cannot lie: His Word and His oath.

You may be familiar with a hymn entitled, "Will Your Anchor Hold in the Storms of Life?" Since coming into an understanding of biblical hope, every time I hear that hymn, I say, "Yes, and the anchor is hope." No hope, no anchor. No hope, no place of refuge. No hope, no Christ in you. No hope, no salvation. It's as important as that.

RETRAINING YOUR MIND

It is vital for our spiritual health and well-being to train our minds according to the Word of God. I know from personal experience that it can be done. For me, the change was like going from night to day. It was a process, but it was worth all the effort I put into it.

As I close this chapter, I want to reemphasize that deliverance will set you free—but it will free you to do your share. Deliverance will not do for you what you can do for yourself. God expects you to do that. This truth applies to the mind, the emotions, and the physical body. Whatever you need deliverance from, if you call upon the name of the Lord, you will be delivered. But, after that, it's your responsibility to conserve your deliverance. And, for many of us, the mind is our most vulnerable place.

I have spent years with missionaries and full-time Christian workers. I would say that one out of five missionaries has a serious problem in the realm of the mind. I can remember missionaries who were qualified, trained, equipped, and dedicated, but who were often laid up for long periods by problems in their minds. Whether you struggle with doubt, unbelief, fear, or despair, God has an answer. The answer is: If you're tormented by a demon, get set free from the demon. But then, remember, that is only the beginning. After that, there is the process of retraining your reactions, your habits, and your thought patterns—bringing every thought into captivity to the obedience of Christ.

When you begin to get restless and edgy, or when you are quick to react in a bad way, stop and ask yourself, "What am I doing wrong? Something has gotten in that shouldn't be there. I'm projecting my mind in the wrong thought channels. I'm beginning to go back on my consecration, my dedication, my faith." When you identify the problem, remember that God has made full spiritual provision.

Ephesians 6:13 says, *"Therefore take up the whole armor of God, that you may be able to withstand in the evil day, and having done all, to stand."* I like that order: First, withstand; then, stand. As I described earlier, every time I made a major new commitment for Christ, the forces of Satan were turned loose against me. This outcome is predictable, and it's one sure sign that I am moving in the will of God. I have learned what to do: withstand—and then, when the storm subsides, I am left standing. The same will be true for you. The ground that you have occupied will be secure under your feet.

Put on the helmet of salvation, and discipline your thoughts in line with the Word of God.

There will always be the need to withstand, and you cannot withstand effectively with an unprotected mind. Take the helmet of salvation, which is the helmet of hope. Put it on, cover your mind, protect your thoughts, and discipline your thoughts in line with the Word of God. The following are some Scriptures to help you to begin to make a habit of renewing your mind through God's Word.

The LORD will give strength to His people; the LORD will bless His people with peace.

(Psalm 29:11)

203

*But I will hope continually, and will praise You
yet more and more. My mouth shall tell of Your
righteousness and Your salvation all the day,
for I do not know their limits. I will go in the
strength of the Lord GOD; I will make mention
of Your righteousness, of Yours only.*

(Psalm 71:14–16)

*Have you not known? Have you not heard? The
everlasting God, the LORD, the Creator of the
ends of the earth, neither faints nor is weary.
His understanding is unsearchable* [There is
no searching of His understanding]. *He gives
power to the weak, and to those who have no
might He increases strength. Even the youths
shall faint and be weary, and the young men
shall utterly fall, but those who wait on the LORD
shall renew their strength; they shall mount up
with wings like eagles, they shall run and not
be weary, they shall walk and not faint.*

(Isaiah 40:28–31)

*Therefore, having been justified by faith, we
have peace with God through our Lord Jesus
Christ, through whom also we have access by
faith into this grace in which we stand, and
rejoice in hope of the glory of God. And not only
that, but we also glory in tribulations, knowing
that tribulation produces perseverance; and*

perseverance, character; and character, hope. Now hope does not disappoint, because the love of God has been poured out in our hearts by the Holy Spirit who was given to us.

(Romans 5:1–5)

I have been crucified with Christ; it is no longer I who live, but Christ lives in me; and the life which I now live in the flesh I live by faith in the Son of God, who loved me and gave Himself for me. (Galatians 2:20)

You are of God, little children, and have overcome them, because He who is in you is greater than he who is in the world. (1 John 4:4)

Be anxious for nothing, but in everything by prayer and supplication, with thanksgiving, let your requests be made known to God; and the peace of God, which surpasses all understanding, will guard your hearts and minds through Christ Jesus. Finally, brethren, whatever things are true, whatever things are noble, whatever things are just, whatever things are pure, whatever things are lovely, whatever things are of good report, if there is any virtue and if there is anything praiseworthy; meditate on these things. (Philippians 4:6–8)

Chapter Eleven

How God Led Me into the Working of Miracles

In this chapter, I want to move forward with a discussion on ministering physical healing and miracles. I concluded chapter eight by saying that unusual miracles were manifest in Paul's ministry. Most of us would be very happy to see ordinary miracles. Whether we receive special miracles may depend on how far we cooperate with the Holy Spirit. Our sensitivity to the Holy Spirit in the realm of healings and miracles sometimes determines the level on which God will work.

TRUST IN GOD'S METHOD OF HEALING

Let me just say that when a gift comes, you either take it or leave it. It is one thing for God the Father to give you a gift. It is another thing for you to receive it. You have to be mentally conditioned and alert to know how to receive what God gives. Otherwise God will give it, but you will miss it.

I want to remind you of one more truth about healing that is very basic. I have prayed for many people over the years and have witnessed many miracles. But I want to encourage you that God does not normally heal everybody by immediate miracles. It is only one of the ways that the Holy Spirit administers what Christ has made available. If you have been praying for healing, or if you have been prayed for and have not received a miracle, don't give up. God loves you. He is on your side. However, you have to remain sensitive to how the Holy Spirit is going to administer to you what you need. He may administer it to one person by an instantaneous, dramatic miracle, and you may be close by and receive nothing miraculous. That doesn't mean that the Lord has written you off or forgotten about you. It just means that you have to take your healing by another route.

God is sovereign. Nobody twists His arm. Do you understand that? We don't tell God how to do it. We try to be sensitive and submissive to the Holy Spirit and let Him do it. However, if you read about some visible miracles, it may change the whole level of your faith. I hope that is what this chapter will do for you.

An Unfolding Ministry

I am now going to share with you some personal testimony, because where I hope to conclude the chapter may be extraordinary to you. If I don't explain it first, then you may not follow along with me or be on board when we get to the end. I will provide some examples from my life for the purpose of building your faith so that by the end of this chapter, you will be mentally prepared to latch on to what God will do for you.

From the year 1943 onward, I believed in divine healing, I believed in divine health, and, by the grace of God, for 95 percent of the time, I essentially enjoyed both healing and health. I give God all the glory for the basic health I have enjoyed. Yet, while I believed in healing, preached it, received it myself through faith in the Word of God, and saw others healed, I had never had much of a ministry of healing.

> **The children had tremendous faith. They expected to be healed, and they got what they expected.**

My first wife, Lydia, had a tremendous ministry in prayer. She brought up a family of orphaned and needy children taken in from other people's homes. During the years she was raising those children, very rarely did they ever go to the doctor. Let me quickly add again that I am not against doctors. I thank God for doctors, nurses, hospitals, and other medical means. But, most times, when the children were sick, they would come to my wife and say, "Pray for me." She would pray, and they would be healed. The children had tremendous faith. They expected to be healed, and they got what they expected. For many years when Lydia and I traveled and ministered, I would say to her, "I'll do the preaching; you pray for the sick." I always thought that was a fair division of labor.

We came to the United States in 1962, and toward the end of that year, we were on the West Coast in Oregon in meetings conducted by Brother Gerald Derstine, a minister of Mennonite background. At the end of the meeting, Lydia and I went up and talked to Brother Derstine and his wife. After a short time of personal fellowship with them, my wife said, "Brother Derstine, would you pray for me?" And he did. When he prayed, Gerald said, "Sister Prince, I have a feeling that God is going to do something new for you very soon." And my wife replied, "Yes, I have that feeling, too." We did not know what that "something new" would be.

Soon after, we moved to Minnesota, where I became associate pastor of an Assemblies of God church in the city of Minneapolis. One morning, my wife and I were praying together, as we normally did at the beginning of the day, and it seemed that the presence of God moved into that room. We both had our arms up in the air, praising God, and when we had finished, my wife turned to me and said, "God has just given me the gift of healing. He put it in my hand." And I replied, "You don't need to tell me. I know it already." How I knew it, I cannot tell you. But I did.

After that time of prayer, Lydia and I went down to the morning prayer meeting in the church, which went from ten o'clock in the morning until twelve noon. At the end of the prayer meeting, a little woman came up to my wife and said, "Sister Prince, I'm not feeling well. Would you pray for me?" Without meditating or reflecting on what had taken place earlier, my wife put out her hand. As she did, the woman went down flat on the floor and stayed there for ten minutes. Afterward, she got up rather apologetically and said, "I'm sorry. I didn't mean to do that. But there was such power, I just couldn't stand up." Lydia and I concluded that something new had indeed taken place.

THE GIFT AT WORK

After that, my wife began to pray for people, and there were quite a number of healings in that assembly. I will relate the results exactly the way they happened. They indicate to me that God has a sense of humor. I can't come to any other conclusion from what I am about to describe. Lydia always said, "It's not I who do it. I stand back and wait for God to direct the gift through me. And when the gift comes, the person either receives it or doesn't receive it. But it's given."

Lydia prayed for many people who were healed, but the gift of healing she received operated differently. The funny thing was that many of the people for whom Lydia prayed at that time would start to jump up and down when the healing gift came— just straight up and down. They don't normally do things like that in Assemblies of God churches, and it was almost embarrassing. But the people who jumped up and down got healed. It's worth jumping up and down to get healed, isn't it? I believe it is worth being thought a fool if you get what you came for. Some people are so dignified that they won't become "foolish," and they don't get what they have come for.

In that church, there was a heavyset, elderly German woman who had a heart condition. She wanted to be prayed for, but she didn't want to be seen jumping up and down. So, she thought she would sneak up on the Lord, which is a very dangerous thing to try. One day, she waited until we were out in the parking lot ready to go home and said, "Sister Prince, would you pray for me?" My wife put out her hand, and this heavy German sister went up and down in the parking lot. She was standing at the door of her car, and her husband could not get her into the car. He got really flustered and said, "What are you doing? If you go on like this, the police will come." That woman got a double dose.

This jumping up and down by people whom Lydia prayed for continued until, after a while, the phenomenon more or less ceased. But it was replaced by what I can only term a kind of "explosion." When Lydia would pray for people, sometimes there would be a very modified explosion, and sometimes there would be quite a loud explosion. My wife and I came to recognize that when the explosion took place, the gift was given. And if the person received it, he or she was healed. Lydia would regularly say to people when they came to her for prayer, "Now listen. I'll ask one thing of you. Stop praying. You have prayed a long while and nothing has happened. Please be quiet and let me pray. And when you get healed, then thank God for it." I saw scores and scores of people healed in that way through my wife's ministry.

As a matter of fact, you may be rather shocked to know that many people pray themselves out of the things they come for. You can pray yourself out of the baptism in the Holy Spirit. You can pray yourself out of deliverance. And you can pray yourself out of healing. Praying is not receiving. Praying is one thing—receiving is another. There is a great spiritual art of receiving. If I go on and on praying, that is sufficient evidence that I have not received, because if I have received, I have no need to continue praying. And if you can stop praying, you might begin receiving. You see, the Lord isn't deaf. When you tell Him you need to be healed, He hears you the first time. And Jesus said, *"When you pray, do not use vain repetitions"* (Matthew 6:7). Going on and on praying can actually be evidence of unbelief.

THE NEED FOR MIRACLES

This healing ministry of Lydia's worked out well. I was quite content, I have to say, with the arrangement of me preaching and Lydia praying for people to be healed. But I saw that although the gift of healing was wonderful, the church also needed the gift of the working of miracles. The church of Jesus Christ collec-

> *I believed that the dramatic, visible manifestation of God's power would do things that could not be done in any other way.*

tively needed this. I believed that the open, dramatic, visible manifestation of God's power would do things that could not be done in any other way. I began to pray that God would restore to the church the gift of the working of miracles as He intended it. If you pray, you had better be prepared to get involved in what you pray for. In due course, God gave me the gift of the working of miracles, though He didn't give it to me in the way I would have expected.

In the paragraphs that follow, I am going to relate how I got involved in the working of miracles. What I am going to tell you may sound extraordinary, but I am going to tell it like it happened.

In June 1970, I had the privilege of being the Bible teacher at the World Conference of the Full Gospel Businessmen's Fellowship, which was conducted in Chicago at the Conrad Hilton Hotel. On the next to last night of the convention, those of us taking part were invited up to the top floor suite, where the Shakarian family was staying. (Demos Shakarian, whose family came to the United States from Armenia, was the founder of the Full Gospel Businessmen's Fellowship.)

Lydia and I went up to the suite, where most of the international directors of the Full Gospel Businessmen's Fellowship, the Shakarian family, and many others had gathered. I knew many of the people in the room personally, including a little man from Oklahoma City. When we arrived, he was in the process of explaining to people that God lengthens legs, and that this happened through his ministry. I stood and listened, but I remained fairly detached. I decided not to be prejudiced on the matter, but to remain open-minded and see if there was something to it or not.

The man from Oklahoma was a quiet, unassuming man, very gentle in his demeanor. He took a lot of time preparing these people, and then he seated them one by one in a chair. He did things in a very orderly fashion. He had a ruler, and he would hold up the legs of the person seated in the chair and measure the difference between them, right down to an eighth of an inch. If he was praying for a woman, he would drape a towel across her knees for modesty. The whole procedure was done decently and in order. As I watched, somebody's leg grew out in front of my eyes. Then another person's leg grew out.

IN THE CHAIR

At that point, I said to my wife, "I think you'd better get into that chair." Lydia sat in the chair, and they held her legs up and measured them. Her left leg was one and one-eighth inches shorter than the right, and she'd had no idea there was any difference in her legs. Often, when people would tell me, "I know my legs are equal," I would simply smile at them because usually they weren't.

That night, in a few seconds, I watched my wife's left leg grow out one and one-eighth inches. When she got out of the chair, she said to me, "You'd better get into that chair."

I said, "Oh, no. There's nothing wrong with me. I don't need to get in the chair."

She replied, "You do."

I protested, "I don't."

She insisted, "You do." So, I got in the chair.

They measured my legs very carefully, and my left leg was a quarter of an inch shorter than my right. As I sat in the chair, I suddenly remembered that my mother had told me that when I was eighteen months old, the doctor had told her that my legs were unequal, and I'd been placed in a splint for a year and a half. Suddenly, I began to see that this was credible. The brother from Oklahoma held my feet, and I felt my left leg grow out. It didn't grow out gradually. It moved out in one single movement. What was particularly noticeable was that it moved from the hip, not from the foot. I knew it had nothing to do with the man who was praying. It was as if an invisible hand had pushed my hip down a quarter of an inch.

I felt my left leg grow out. It didn't grow out gradually. It moved out in one single movement.

At that time, I had thought I was a fit, healthy person. But you can get so used to certain conditions you live with that you don't consider them to be abnormal. I realized that if I would stand and preach for an hour, I would get a kind of burning sensation across the small of my back. After my leg grew out (unfortunately for my congregations), I could stand for three hours without getting the pain.

I am just relating the results of this encounter objectively. By that time, my wife and I had been married for about twenty-five years, but we had never been able to walk together because her stride was so short that I could not accommodate myself to it. I would walk ahead, then walk back to her, and then walk ahead again. People would often say, "What's the matter with you two? Have you quarreled?"

The day after this prayer session, when Lydia and I took a walk, her stride was 50 percent longer than it had been, without her realizing it. She didn't think about it consciously; it just happened. Second, she was so used to having to push her left leg to make up for the difference in length that when it was lengthened, she still pushed it down as we walked—and bruised the heel on that foot. This is just to show you how absolutely objective it is and how unconnected it is with reasoning processes.

"I Can Do That!"

While I stood there that particular night watching this leg lengthening as it happened, something inside me said, "You can do that!" And I blurted out:

"You know, I think I can do that." Brother Demos Shakarian turned to me and said, "Of course, you can do that, Brother Prince." I thought in response, *It isn't as obvious as that.* However, something started moving in me.

Earlier that year, I had received a letter from John Beckett, a friend of mine from Elyria, Ohio. John is a very successful businessman, the president of his own corporation, and a graduate in engineering from the Massachusetts Institute of Technology. In other words, he's not a kook but a well-rounded Christian. John related to me in the letter that at a recent weekend convention, some sixty or seventy people had had their legs grow out in response to prayer. In many cases, this result had been associated with the healing of other maladies, such as arthritis. Through this report and other encounters, I was already somewhat mentally conditioned to move forward in this area of ministry.

Then, in August 1970, I was one of three or four teachers in a Layman's Training Institute on the island of Jamaica. Brother Charles Simpson was one of the other teachers, and Brother Don Basham was another. John Beckett was one of the laymen who came to Jamaica to be trained. He had not been there twenty-four hours before legs were growing out right and left in response to prayer.

Again and again, I watched people who didn't believe it was going to happen experience its reality. The woman proprietor of the hotel sat down in the chair and gasped with amazement when her own leg grew out. It spread almost like an epidemic. I was sitting by the swimming pool one night when one of the laymen went up to the night watchman, who was a native Jamaican, and said, "If you see a miracle happen before your eyes, will you confess that Jesus Christ is Lord?" The poor man really didn't know what to say, so the layman sat him down in a chair and measured his legs. One was shorter than the other, and it grew out. John Beckett went down into the city port of Montego Bay to get his hair cut, and the barber ended up in the chair having his leg lengthened.

"If you see a miracle happen before your eyes, will you confess that Jesus Christ is Lord?"

After this had been going on for a while, John Beckett said to me, "If you're going to start doing this, you'd better start while we've got any customers left. We're running out of patients." And really we were. It was difficult to find anybody left in that area who still had unequal legs.

John found a woman and seated her in the chair for me to pray for her. Then, he said, "Now the real tricky thing is how to hold the people's feet. When you've got that, the rest follows." I hoped he was right, and I held the woman's feet in the prescribed way. As I knelt in front of her, sweating profusely, the woman's leg grew out rather slowly and stubbornly. It moved about half an inch. I knew I had gotten it, but rather uncertainly.

A BREAKTHROUGH

After that conference, I had to go home to England. My mother had died earlier in the year, and I had a number of personal matters to attend to while there. I returned to the United States just in time to be one of the teachers at the Tennessee CFO, a charismatic teaching conference in Eatonton, Georgia. The first morning I was there, I did not feel adequate or ready to minister to people. Actually, I felt that I was the one who needed to receive ministry. So, I went out in the forest by myself and got alone with God. I prostrated myself on the ground on my face before the Lord, and I asked God to search me and to cleanse me and renew me and make me fit to minister to people. As I prayed, I asked God to show me if there was anything in me that would be a hindrance to His work, and something very strange happened. As I lay there before the Lord, one very clear word formed in my mind: *embarrassment.*

By that time, I had been in the ministry of deliverance for many years, and I realized that this was the name of a spirit. *Embarrassment?* I thought to myself, *I don't have embarrassment.* Then I remembered how, all my life, I had been afraid of any kind of public scene. Even when I was six or seven years old, if my mother went into a store to argue with the shopkeeper, I would say, "You go in, but I'm staying outside. I won't get involved in that." Looking back over my life by the inspiration of the Holy Spirit, I saw how I had actually charted my course to always avoid public embarrassment and confrontation. When you are a preacher, that is quite a lot of pressure, because a preacher is right out in public.

"Lord," I said, "if there is this spirit of embarrassment in me, I don't want it." Immediately, I felt it leave me. I knew I had been released from it. Sensing an assurance of cleansing, renewal, and empowerment from God, I got up and went back to the camp. I knew I was ready.

WHERE TO BEGIN?

Concerning this ministry of leg lengthening, I prayed, "God, if You want me to get into this, You have to show me where to begin. I'm not going to begin until I have direct guidance from You." That day, I sat at the lunch table next to a young man named Paul Petrie, whom I knew quite well, and who is in full-time ministry. I was telling him about wrestling with the issue of this ministry, and he said, "Well, Brother Prince, you'd better begin with me."

"What's the matter with you?" I asked.

He said, "I'm crooked all over. One leg is shorter than the other, one arm is shorter than the other." Then he added, "There's my teeth, too."

I asked, "What's the matter with your teeth?"

He pulled down his lower lip and showed me. "You can see the lower row is totally uneven. Some are up, some down, some forward, some back."

His invitation really wasn't very welcome to me. Even so, I said, "Well, let's begin with your leg, anyhow." I seated him in a chair in the middle of the dining room and lifted up his legs. There was more than an inch difference, and his short leg grew out instantly. Somewhat encouraged, I said, "Now, we'll try your arms." I stood him straight against a post in the middle of the dining hall, and then got him to swing his arms and bring them up, with his palms together. There was well over an inch difference between his arms, too. Instantly, the short arm grew out.

Honestly, I would have been quite content to stop there, but Paul said, "What about my teeth?" *After all that*, I thought to myself, *I can't really say no at this point.* So I told Paul, "We'll see what God will do. Close your mouth." Then I placed my hands on his cheeks, and I prayed until I felt somehow that I was in contact with God. I thought to myself, *I'd better strengthen his faith.* So I asked, "Did you feel anything in your mouth? Did it feel kind of full?" Paul replied, "Yes, it did." "Well," I said, "maybe God is doing something."

By that time, people were coming from everywhere. They began to line up, so that I spent the next twenty minutes with people in and out of that chair, legs and arms growing out just as quickly as they could. Before long, I had to go off to an appointment in another part of the camp. But as I was on my way there, Paul Petrie's wife, Becky, came running after me, all out of breath.

"Do you want to see Paul's teeth?" she asked.

"Why, what's happened to them?" I replied.

"They're absolutely straight," she answered.

"Then," I said, "I definitely do."

We went back to where Paul was, and I looked at his teeth. The lower row of teeth was completely even; the teeth were neither up nor down, forward nor back. Then Paul said to me, "They still need capping." So I said, "I think we'll leave that to the Lord."

LAUNCHED!

That was how I was launched in the ministry of lengthening legs and arms. At that one camp, I must have prayed for over two hundred people, and legs and arms grew out. Additional things happened as well. Deaf ears were opened. Other miracles and healings took place.

After a while, people said, "If it's that easy, we can do it," and, praise the Lord, they could! That's the good thing about it—there's no monopoly on it, believe me.

Right in the midst of this, some of my well-meaning friends said to me, in so many words, "You know, for a rather well-known, scholarly Bible teacher to go around kneeling on the floor, holding people's legs, isn't exactly very dignified. How do you know you're not getting off on a tangent? How do you know this is from God?"

Those questions rather disturbed me. In response, my first thought was: *I'll take this a little slowly. I'll play it a little cool and see how it will work out.* I began to seek God, and He answered me very clearly. I did not hear Him answer in an audible voice, but He said to me, "I have given you a gift, and you can do two things with it. You can use it and it will increase, or you can fail to use it and lose it." The Lord also gave me the Scripture, *"For whoever has, to him more will be given, and he will have abundance; but whoever does not have, even what he has will be taken away"* (Matthew 13:12). In response, I said, "Lord, I'll use it. I don't care what people think. I've been controversial before. I may be controversial again. But I will use it." And I did. Many people have lost spiritual gifts by ignoring them and being afraid to use them. If God gives me an ability to help people, I know I'm answerable in two directions—I'm answerable to God, and I'm answerable to the people.

Gradually, God has honored His promise. He has given me more and more. The more I use it, and the more I testify of it, the bolder I am. The more I put God on the spot, the more God comes up with the answer.

> *God has honored His promise. He has given me more and more.*

In our next chapter, you will see God's miracle power in a very practical application.

Chapter Twelve

Going into Action!

I am going to give you a few basic principles regarding preparation for healing, and then I am going to allow you to "look in" on a time of actual ministry.

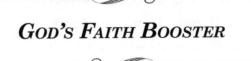

GOD'S FAITH BOOSTER

The basic principles I will share are very important, so I want you to pay careful attention to them. For many centuries, the faith of the Christian church has been on such a pathetically low level that God has to come to our help. I have been with Christians who have been faithful members of their churches for over twenty years but have never in their lives witnessed one visible miracle. That is why I call this unusual ministry of lengthening arms and legs "God's Faith Booster." When NASA wanted to send a satellite into orbit, they had to have a booster rocket to get it out of the earth's atmosphere and beyond the field of gravity. Once it was in orbit, it just kept circling as long as NASA wanted it to.

This simple, visible miracle of leg or arm lengthening, which you can see and feel in your own body, is

God's booster for your faith. It will get you out of the pull of gravity and into orbit. That is what God will do for you. Often, I would pray for people who said, "I don't believe." I would reply, "It doesn't matter. I do. It'll happen. But when it happens, when you're in orbit, then it is your responsibility." In addition, I would say, "Don't come back in reentry too soon. Stay in orbit until you have all you need. When God's power moves into your leg or arm, and you see it at work, open up and let every single area of your body get healed."

It matters a great deal that we have the right attitude. You may have fifteen different ailments, but that is the time to get healed. If you stay in orbit long enough, you will come back whole. If you come back in reentry too soon, you will get only a little.

It is rather laughable, but people have come up to me and said, "You know, Brother Prince, my leg grew out an inch. But I didn't get healed of my eyesight." It is amusing to me that people would say, "The only thing that happened to me was that my leg grew out one inch," because, years ago, before this ministry began, nobody would have talked that way. They would have said, "Do you know what happened to me? My leg grew out an inch!"

Let me characterize this leg-lengthening miracle in another way. When this miracle takes place in your body, you are plugged into the power outlet. Now you know the power is flowing. My advice is, "Stay plugged in until you have all you need. Don't take the plug out too soon!" You'll never have as good an opportunity as the moment when God's miracle-working power is in your body.

> **You'll never have as good an opportunity as the moment when God's miracle-working power is in your body.**

You may ask, "How do I stay plugged in?" My answer is this: not by praying, but by thanking. All you have to do is relax. Don't try to create something. You can't do it by trying. Relax, and let the Lord do the miracle. Then, keep on thanking Him. All of us owe God half a billion thanks. Let's start paying it off. Much more is received by thanking than by praying.

TESTIMONIES OF HEALING

Let me now give you some examples to show you what I mean. In September 1970, I was the Bible teacher in the regional convention of the Full Gospel Businessmen's Fellowship in Charlotte, North Carolina. Kathryn Kuhlman had been there the previous day, and the meeting room of the hotel was absolutely packed, with six or seven hundred people attending. I was conducting the last service, and, without having planned it, I began to talk about people's legs growing out. After that, it didn't matter what I talked about. Lengthening of legs is what people wanted. At the end of my presentation, I was surrounded by a horde of people asking me to pray for them. So, I sat them down and began to pray.

An Unexpected Ministry

Some months later, I was with Brother Demos Shakarian in Chicago, and he told me a story about that meeting I had never heard from him before. He said, "At that same meeting where you shared, I saw that you would never be able to pray for all the people who were waiting for prayer, and somebody came up to me and asked, 'Do you lengthen legs, Brother Shakarian?'" Demos added, "That was the one thing I never wanted to get involved in, but the man insisted that I take his legs and pray. To my amazement, the leg grew out." Then, he said, "Brother Prince, you didn't know it, but I was there in that ballroom from 10:00 p.m. to 1:00 a.m., praying for people's legs." The ballroom was so crowded and so much was going on that it was impossible to keep track of things, and I had no idea he was there praying for people.

God's Operating Table

I myself was there from ten o'clock until midnight. I was walking out into the foyer of the hotel, and there was still a line of people, but I said, "Midnight. Shop closed. I'm going to bed." A woman who was standing in the line right beside me got very indignant. She said, "I've stood here waiting one hour to be prayed for. Are you going to bed without praying for me?" So I replied, "Sit down and don't talk." She sat down and I picked up her legs. One was shorter than the other, and it immediately grew out. I said, "Good night; I'm going to bed," and vanished up to my room.

> **"I was continuously under the power of God. At the end of that time, my spine was absolutely straight."**

About a month later, I received a letter from this woman. She began by saying, "You won't remember me," and then proceeded to describe herself and the situation until I knew who she was. She went on, "You never gave me time to tell you, but when you prayed for me, I had a severe double curvature of the spine. After my leg grew out, I was on God's operating table for forty-eight hours. I was continuously under the power of God. At the end of that time, my spine was absolutely straight." That is a perfect example of staying plugged in. She didn't do that because I instructed her, because, by the time I prayed for her, I was tired of the business at hand. But she did, in fact, stay plugged into the power of the Lord, and she received a remarkable healing.

A Brand-New Kneecap

The year after the events I just described, I was in the spring Tennessee CFO Camp—the same place where I had launched this ministry. I got involved every night in praying for people. Legs grew out, arms grew out, and then, on the basis of these results, other miracles followed. In that camp, there was a woman who had had one kneecap surgically removed, and she saw all that was happening. I never prayed for her, but she went back to her cabin, and the other three ladies in her cabin prayed for her. Twenty-four hours later, she had a completely new kneecap. She normally wore her dresses a little longer than the average length in order to conceal the missing kneecap. It was rather comical because, when the Lord gave her a new kneecap, she was so proud of it that she turned up the hem of her dress to show it off.

This same woman was in a meeting in Arlington, Virginia, later that year, where I happened to be the speaker. The meeting was in an Episcopal church, and she came forward and gave her testimony in person and let everybody look at the kneecap. At that meeting, I asked her, "What happened when those ladies prayed for your kneecap? Did you get any immediate results?" She replied, "At first, I just felt a beautiful, warm glow in the knee. But I went on praising God, and twenty-four hours later, I had the kneecap."

That woman was spiritually minded. Many people would have felt the warm glow, looked down, seen that the knee was the same, and said, "Nothing happened." They would have taken the plug out at that point and received no more. Do you follow what I am saying? Instead, she stayed plugged in, and that is the key. It is setting your mind that when the power of God begins to work, you continue so that you can get what you need.

An Unplanned Message

A few months after that, I was with Brother Demos Shakarian again at the Full Gospel Businessmen's regional convention in Chicago. I was the banquet speaker on the last night of the convention, and I had a message all prepared on praying for the government. In all humility, I was really going to give it to them! It was just a month before the national election, and I had what I was going to share all lined up in my mind.

Contrary to plan, I started to speak about legs. Once I get on that topic, there is no turning back. You just can't go in any other direction. In the middle of my message, Demos got up and told the incident about the scene in the ballroom at the Charlotte meeting. So, at the end of my sharing, I said, "Now we'll do it. Demos, you take one chair over there, and I'll take one chair on this side." It seems the more nerve you have, the more God backs you up. The first person Demos prayed for was a chiropractor, and his leg grew out. From then on, he was our cheerleader. He would stand up there and say, "It's growing out. The ankle's turning. I can see it." A little while later, the chiropractor's wife came and got in my chair for prayer. I don't know exactly what was wrong with her, but I just held her legs, and whatever happened, it was exactly what she needed. When she knew she was healed (and the chiropractor was watching all the time), she got up from the chair, pointed at her husband, and said, "From now on, you're fired!"

The Presence of the Spirit of Miracles

I was at a meeting at a Hilton Hotel in New Orleans. We were ministering the lengthening of legs and arms, and a number of miracles took place. A woman came up to me and said, "Pray for my leg." I asked, "What's the matter?" and she said, "I had polio as a child, and my left leg is three inches shorter than my right." So I said, "All right, sit down."

She was wearing boots that came up just below the knee, partly to conceal the inequality in her legs, I suppose. I lifted up her legs and measured them carefully—and they were exactly *equal*. So, I said, "I can't pray for you; your legs are equal." She said, "Impossible! My left leg is three inches shorter than my right!" "Well," I said, "just look." She looked down and then tore her boots off—I mean, she flung them off. Then, she said, "Measure without boots!" I did, and her legs were exactly equal. Suddenly, she realized what had happened, and she let out a scream. She said, "Where's my husband? I've got to tell him!"

What had the Lord done? He had lengthened her left leg three inches without her being prayed for, and without her knowing what had happened. That is the Spirit of Miracles, and it can hover over a place. If we will move with God, there's no limit to what He can do.

> *If we will move with God, there's no limit to what He can do.*

When I was ministering in Shreveport, Louisiana, a woman came up to me and said, "You may not remember me, but you prayed for my daughter in Mobile, Alabama. She had polio. Her legs were unequal, and her leg grew out. But while you were praying for my daughter, God healed my brain injury. I didn't even ask Him to do it, and I didn't realize it had happened until I walked out later."

There will come a moment when the Spirit of Miracles is here, and you can receive your healing. We have to be sensitive and receptive and responsive.

Receiving the "Package Deal"

In an earlier chapter, I mentioned that I was ministering in a Methodist church in Falls Church,

Virginia, and a woman came up to me who was a judge and a member of the supreme court of the State of Virginia. She said to me, "Brother Prince, can you help me? I have been in continual pain for ten years, night and day. I've never been without pain, and no pain reliever touches my condition." I asked, "What's wrong with you?" She'd had an intestinal problem for ten years, and she started to give me a list of maladies. Finally, I said, "Just leave it. You need the package deal."

Then, I told her this: "When we start praying for people, don't get in the chair immediately. Stand close and watch what God is doing until your faith is built up. When you feel ready, sit down in the chair." After about twenty minutes, I asked, "Are you ready?" She said, "I am." I said, "This is it. You are now going to get the package deal." As she sat in the chair, I lifted her legs, and they were indeed unequal. The short leg grew out, and I stepped back to watch. For about ten or fifteen minutes, a small group of us, including my wife, stood around and watched God operate on her body. You could actually see the part of her body that was being affected by the Holy Spirit. He went over her area by area. At the end of about fifteen minutes, she was apparently completely healed. God completely restored her whole interior. She told me personally that God's power had zapped her, and she was out of this world for forty-five minutes. When she came to, she was free of pain for the first time in ten years.

Later, she discovered that when her intestines had been operated on, doctors had put in metal clips to hold things in place. When God healed her, He removed the clips. There was no longer any evidence of them.

This woman is a very bold person and a well-known personality where she lives. She tells the story everywhere. I met her a few years later in Ardmore, Oklahoma, and she said, "Brother Prince, you can tell my story anywhere." My wife Lydia asked her, "What was it like when God healed you?" This woman has a very vivid way of speaking, and she replied, "It was just as if fifteen plumbers moved into my stomach and started joining up the pipes."

Crippling Arthritis Healed

Shortly after that meeting, I traveled to Spain, where I was speaking to a mixed community of Scandinavians, Dutch, English, and many others, and most of them were not by any means charismatic. It took me three mornings to get to this topic, and I had to introduce it very slowly. The third morning of the meetings, God moved in and zapped them. One woman, a matron from an English hospital, had

> *One woman was so crippled with arthritis that she was unable to bend. God healed her completely.*

been a nurse for forty years. She was so crippled with arthritis that she was unable to bend. I just held her leg briefly and it quickly grew out. Then, God healed her completely. After the prayer, she bent over, touched her toes, and moved her back. One testimony from a person like that, and you are convinced. It breaks down all the reserve, uncertainty, and doubt. And God did many more amazing miracles in Spain.

Curvature of the Spine Healed

Nothing fascinates me more than to see God operating on a body. There was one Englishwoman whom I would estimate was about forty years old. I didn't know what was wrong with her, so she started telling me everything. Finally, I said, as I had said to the woman healed of constant pain, "You need the package deal. Let's leave it at that." When I prayed for her, her leg immediately grew out, and I knew something was going to happen. At that point, I just stepped back to see what God would do. She had curvature of the spine, among other things, and that curvature also affected her rib cage. Actually, her healing was very comical. She looked like one of those dolls that, when you pull a string, the arm jerks, and when you pull it again, the leg jerks. She was sitting there for ten minutes with that happening. We just stood there and watched. Nobody touched her. At the end of that time, she was completely healed. She told us the next day that her spine was straight, her ribs were straight, and everything was in its right place.

Lost Years Restored by God

I want to preface the next miraculous testimony with a Scripture. The Lord said through the prophet Joel,

> *The threshing floors shall be full of wheat, and the vats shall overflow with new wine and oil. So I will restore to you the years that the swarming locust has eaten, the crawling locust, the consuming locust, and the chewing locust.*
>
> (Joel 2:24–25)

I used to think that this passage said, "I will drive the locusts out." But it says more than that. It says, "I will restore to you the years that they have eaten." The Lord made this truth real to me when I prayed for a woman in Birmingham, Alabama. We were having a meeting of the Full Gospel Businessmen's Fellowship at which God was lengthening people's legs, and I was telling the people, "Get the package deal. Don't just get your leg lengthened, but when that happens, get everything."

A woman came up, and I don't think she knew very much about what was going on. She was rather a pathetic sight. She had some disease that was breaking down her bones. Her left leg and arm were partially paralyzed. The muscles of her face were paralyzed on that side, also, so that her face was crooked, and she literally couldn't smile. Her face was the color of parchment, and she looked about as miserable as anybody could look. She started to tell me all the things that were wrong with her, and I said, "Please stop, because I can't remember it all. We'll see what God will do."

I prayed for her, and I could not tell you whether I had faith or not. But I felt the sense of God's power and presence come over her, and I stepped back and did no more. For the next ten minutes, a little group of us stood and watched God totally renew that woman. Her skin changed, and, apparently, her bone structure must have been repaired because, at the end of ten minutes, she could use her left leg and arm

In ten minutes, God had blotted out ten years of this woman's sickness, suffering, and tragedy.

freely, and she was able to smile. A woman who was standing there and who knew her and had come with her said, "You look just like you used to look ten years ago!" In ten minutes, God had blotted out ten years of this woman's sickness, suffering, and tragedy. That's what God means when He says, "I will restore to you the years that the locust has eaten." It's not just getting rid of the locusts—which would be wonderful in itself—but it's undoing what they did. Psalm 103:5 says, *"Who satisfies your mouth with good things, so that your youth is renewed like the eagle's."*

Having read these stories, you should not only be ready for your own healing, but also inspired to pray for the healing of other people as well.

AN ACTUAL HEALING SERVICE

Editor's Note: God uses various methods in healing, as have been described in this book. What follows is one of those ways. It is a transcript of a service Derek conducted with a congregation of six hundred people. As Derek has said, "This is not a gimmick, and it's not a game. It is the exercise of a spiritual gift." As you read, imagine yourself there, watching Derek minister to those present, an eyewitness to legs and arms growing out. Then, envision yourself sitting in the chair, receiving all that God has for you.

What I want you to do now is cooperate with me. Now, I'm going to ask you to give me two chairs. There's one there. If you put that one there, this way, and we'll have one there, the opposite way, a little closer here. Thank you. That's fine. All right.

Now, the more people who witness from close quarters, the better pleased I am. I particularly enjoy having children there. I've had children with their noses about half an inch from somebody's heel when it grew out, because I reckon that when a child sees a few legs grow out, it doesn't matter what the teacher in school says, that child will know forever there's a God.

All right, now the ground rules. One thing I ask for is discipline. The Holy Spirit is not the author of confusion. If we get confused and undisciplined, He departs; and, without Him, we get nothing. We have to be cooperative with the Holy Spirit.

The second thing is that I ask you to allow me to have the absolute prerogative of who sits in the chair. I want no one to come and sit in the chair unless I personally invite them to come, because it's important that I begin with the right people. My faith begins on a certain level. When I start, I have faith for some things and not for others, so I begin with the easy cases. And when those are working, then faith mounts in people and in me. But if I pick a lemon to start with, then we're all back. It takes a long while to get over a bad start. I did it once in a Presbyterian church in Pittsburgh—and, well, we won't go into that, but it taught me a lesson.

Now, the other thing is the behavior of the congregation. As I said before, I want you to understand this is not a one-person ministry. It is the body ministering

241

to the body. And I want everybody who is a believer here to be prayerful and worshipful and thankful. The more we can have an atmosphere of praise and worship and thankfulness, the more the Holy Spirit will work.

This is always a step into the unknown. I never know what will happen. I just step out and hope that God is there to catch me. As a matter of fact, He may let you get about two inches from the concrete, but He does catch you. Let me say, also, I am no medical practitioner. I'm a preacher of the gospel. I respect chiropractors, physicians, surgeons, dentists. I've had the privilege of praying for at least half a dozen chiropractors, and every one of them has acknowledged a real miracle. So, I want you to understand I'm not in competition. We're all on the same team, but we're working in different places.

Now, I would like to begin with somebody who has a medically diagnosed inequality of the legs and doesn't want it any longer. You have a medically diagnosed inequality? Who diagnosed it? How much is it? You are a good one to start with. You want to get rid of it? Good. All right. Which leg is it? Right leg. Hold on a moment. Your right leg is short. Is that right? (Yes, sir.)

Okay. Sit down. Now I've put him there because hopefully you can see the leg grow. Now, if you've got fifteen other ailments, settle for the package deal. Okay? I'll hold your legs up. You're right. It's about an inch and a half. Thank You, Lord. Can you feel that growing now? (Yes, sir.)

Okay. Let's give the Lord a praise offering. Hallelujah! Glory to God. Thank You, Lord. Thank You, Jesus. Glory to Your name, Lord. We praise You and thank You. Bless Your name. Amen. Hallelujah. Glory to God.

God will do something more for you, brother. Just sit there. You're getting an overall treatment. Now, this is where we just worship the Lord quietly, because we're cooperating with the Lord.

Thank You, Jesus. We give You the praise, Lord. We give You the glory. All right.

Do we have anybody else with a similar type complaint of unequal legs? That man there. You're just praising the Lord. Well, that's a good thing to do. We don't want to quench that. There must be several other people. You have unequal legs? How do you know? You don't have a build up, a support. No. All right. You're the one we want. Could you come up and sit in this chair, please? You have back problems continually? Now, when the leg grows out, settle for it. Your back problems are finished. You need a package deal? You'll get it, too.

Now, I want to say something else. All this I've learned by experience. It's not medical theory. But frequently, the short leg will grow out beyond the long one, sometimes as much as half an inch or an inch.

Then the other leg will grow out to equalize. Now, I understand that it's not really the legs that are growing, but the adjustment is taking place in the spine, and it is visible in the legs. And if you have spinal curvature, this is normal. The way the healing will take place is that the short leg will grow out beyond the long one, the long will then catch up to the short leg, and sometimes it will go on maybe three or four times. This is not a gimmick. It is not necessarily any change in the real length of the legs, but it's the manifestation of what's taking place in the spine. You see, the two main ways that we can see what's happened in the spine is through the legs and through the arms. And when those change without you doing it, it is your spine that's being adjusted.

Okay. Can you scoot back in the chair? Well, this is your right leg, and it's a good inch short. Do you see that? Do you feel it growing now? All right. Stay there and get the package deal. Praise the Lord. That's right. It's coming. Just move around. The Holy Spirit is going to move your spine for you. Just yield to it. Don't fight it. Well, I think He hasn't finished. You said you wanted the package deal. You'd better get it. Just fix your mind on the Lord. Keep praising Him and thanking Him.

Thank You, Jesus; praise Your name.

That's it. Something's happening now. That's right. I told you. Don't fight against it. That's the Holy Spirit. He's the best chiropractor in the world. That's right.

Thank You, Lord. Thank You, Jesus. Let's all worship the Lord. It's not altogether easy for somebody to let go in front of everybody. Hallelujah. Thank You, Jesus. That's right. Glory to God. Hallelujah. You're going to have a straight spine when you're finished.

See what I mean by the Lord operating? It's got nothing to do with me. I'm not there; I'm not touching the person, but God is doing it. Amen. Thank You, God. Praise Your wonderful name. Glory to God. We give You the praise and the glory in the name of Jesus.

This woman here says she's burning up. You see, that's God's healing power. Many people talk about a burning feeling, and that is the healing presence of God. Now, let's rejoice, but let's also keep reverent because this is a very precious and wonderful thing that God is doing. Amen. Now, do you think you're ready to go back? You just need to stay plugged in. I think in a little while you won't have the deformity.

Okay. All right. We'll get somebody else in your chair. What's your problem? Your left leg is a quarter inch shorter than the other. How do you know? Okay. Do you want to be changed? It's too late once it's happened. There was one man who didn't want it to happen because it would mean readjusting the legs of all his pants, and he didn't want that. Okay.

Can you scoot back in the chair? It's your left leg that's short about a half an inch and growing rapidly. Amen. Well beyond. You're getting a back adjustment of some kind. Thank You, Lord. Just sit there and thank Him. We thank You, Lord. We praise You. Hallelujah. We praise Your name. Thank You, Lord. Amen.

Proclamation: Overcoming by the Blood and the Word

I am sure that when the Israelites were first delivered from slavery in Egypt, they concluded that, now, all their troubles were over—that the rest of their journey to the Promised Land would be easy and uneventful. As a result, they were unprepared for what lay ahead, and they failed to continue trusting God for strength, help, and deliverance. The same is often true for us after God has given us freedom. We think the rest of our lives should be easy and uneventful.

GOD IS NEVER UNPREPARED FOR THE CHALLENGES WE FACE

The fact that God has given you a tremendous deliverance, victory, blessing, or healing—whatever it may be—does not mean that you won't experience further testing in some way. The greater the victory, the greater the test that you will be able to face on the basis of that victory. The Israelites thought that because they'd had this remarkable deliverance, nothing else could happen that would ever challenge their faith. They couldn't conceive that any such challenge could happen when God was personally leading them, and when He had just granted them such a wonderful victory. Consequently, they weren't ready when they came to the bitter pool—and that is why they began to murmur and complain.

God is never confronted with a situation that He doesn't have an answer to.

No matter how many times we may feel unprepared, however, God is never unprepared. God never has an emergency. He is never confronted with a situation that He doesn't have an answer to. As you have relied on Him for your healing or miracle, continue relying on Him for health and deliverance. *"Trust in Him at all times, you people; pour out your heart before Him; God is a refuge for us"* (Psalm 62:8).

Hold on to the freedom you have gained through continual faith in God's Word. Then, in each new test or challenge, keep on trusting Him, believing His Word, making confessions in regard to its truth, taking action on it—and giving thanks. This is how you can continually move in the will and power of God for whatever is needed in your life, whether it is health, healing, deliverance, or victory.

A DAILY PROCLAMATION OF HEALTH AND HEALING

In Revelation 12:11, we have a picture, I believe, of the tremendous, end-time conflict between the people of God and the people of Satan. The devil himself is personally involved. Yet this verse also gives us the key to victory:

> *They* [the people of God] *overcame him* [Satan] *by the blood of the Lamb and by the word of their testimony, and they did not love their lives to the death.*

How do we overcome Satan? *"By the blood of the Lamb and by the word of* [our] *testimony."* We overcome Satan when we testify personally to what the Bible, the Word of God, says the blood of Jesus does for us. You must first know what the Word of God says. Then, you need to make it personal, applying it in your own life.

My wife, Ruth, and I have a form of testimony that we regularly use, which is based on the Word of God. I encourage you to make it your daily confession:

My body is a temple for the Holy Spirit; redeemed, cleansed, and sanctified by the blood of Jesus. My members, the parts of my body, are instruments of righteousness yielded to God for His service and for His glory. The devil has no place in me, no power over me, no unsettled claims against me. All has been settled by the blood of Jesus. I overcome Satan by the blood of the Lamb and the word of my testimony, and I love not my life unto the death. My body is for the Lord, and the Lord is for my body.

Every one of the above statements is taken from the Bible:

"My body is a temple for the Holy Spirit."
(See 1 Corinthians 3:16; 6:19.)

"Redeemed, cleansed, and sanctified by the blood of Jesus."
(See, for example, Hebrews 9:14; 13:12; 1 Peter 1:18–19; 1 John 1:7; Revelation 5:9.)

"My members, the parts of my body, are instruments of righteousness yielded to God for His service and for His glory." (See Romans 6:13.)

"The devil has no place in me, no power over me, no unsettled claims against me."
(See, for example, Luke 10:18–19; Acts 10:38; 2 Thessalonians 3:3; Revelation 12:10.)

"All has been settled by the blood of Jesus."
(See, for example, Colossians 1:19–20;
Hebrews 2:14–15; 7:26–27; 10:10.)

"I overcome Satan by the blood of the Lamb and the word of my testimony, and I love not my life unto the death."
(See Revelation 12:11.)

"My body is for the Lord, and the Lord is for my body." (See 1 Corinthians 6:13.)

You need to make this your personal confession, not just a repetition of what Ruth and I say. You are saying it because the Bible says it. If you believe the Bible, you believe these words. Say it out loud now—and every day. You are talking into the unseen spiritual world, and there is where your words have an impact that you cannot even begin to measure.

> **The unseen spiritual world is where your words have an impact that you cannot even begin to measure.**

If you really believe this confession, then give thanks to the Lord. That is the expression of your faith.

CONTINUALLY OVERCOMING

Earlier in this book, we talked about how Exodus 15:26, *"I am the LORD who heals you,"* is in the continuous present tense: "I am the Lord who is healing you." If you are living in contact with the Lord, He is healing you all the time. It is a continual process. Likewise, no matter what situation you may face—a need for healing, deliverance, peace of mind, or a miraculous intervention—as you live in contact with the Lord, He is continually enabling you to overcome.

These things I have spoken to you, that in Me you may have peace. In the world you will have tribulation; but be of good cheer, I have overcome the world. (John 16:33)

You are of God, little children, and have overcome them, because He who is in you is greater than he who is in the world. (1 John 4:4)

May God bless you as you come to know Him as your personal Healer and Deliverer.

About the Author

Derek Prince (1915–2003) was born in India of British parents. He was educated as a scholar of Greek and Latin at Eton College and King's College, Cambridge, in England. Upon graduation, he held a fellowship (equivalent to a professorship) in Ancient and Modern Philosophy at King's College. Prince also studied Hebrew, Aramaic, and modern languages at Cambridge and the Hebrew University in Jerusalem. As a student, he was a philosopher and self-proclaimed agnostic.

While in the British Medical Corps during World War II, Prince began to study the Bible as a philosophical work. Converted through a powerful encounter with Jesus Christ, he was baptized in the Holy Spirit a few days later. Out of this encounter, he formed two conclusions: first, that Jesus Christ is alive; second, that the Bible is a true, relevant, up-to-date book. These conclusions altered the whole course of his life, which he then devoted to studying and teaching the Bible as the Word of God.

Discharged from the army in Jerusalem in 1945, he married Lydia Christensen, founder of a children's home there. Upon their marriage, he immediately became father to Lydia's eight adopted daughters—six Jewish, one Palestinian Arab, and one English. Together, the family saw the rebirth of the state of Israel in 1948. In the late 1950s, they adopted another daughter while Prince was serving as principal of a teacher training college in Kenya.

In 1963, the Princes immigrated to the United States and pastored a church in Seattle. In 1973, Prince became one of the founders of Intercessors for America. His book *Shaping History through Prayer and Fasting* has awakened

Christians around the world to their responsibility to pray for their governments. Many consider underground translations of the book as instrumental in the fall of communist regimes in the USSR, East Germany, and Czechoslovakia.

Lydia Prince died in 1975, and Prince married Ruth Baker (a single mother to three adopted children) in 1978. He met his second wife, like his first wife, while she was serving the Lord in Jerusalem. Ruth died in December 1998 in Jerusalem, where they had lived since 1981.

Until a few years before his own death in 2003 at the age of eighty-eight, Prince persisted in the ministry God had called him to as he traveled the world, imparting God's revealed truth, praying for the sick and afflicted, and sharing his prophetic insights into world events in the light of Scripture. Internationally recognized as a Bible scholar and spiritual patriarch, Derek Prince established a teaching ministry that spanned six continents and more than sixty years. He is the author of more than fifty books, six hundred audio teachings, and one hundred video teachings, many of which have been translated and published in more than one hundred languages. He pioneered teaching on such groundbreaking themes as generational curses, the biblical significance of Israel, and demonology.

Prince's radio program, which began in 1979, has been translated into more than a dozen languages and continues to touch lives. Derek's main gift of explaining the Bible and its teaching in a clear and simple way has helped build a foundation of faith in millions of lives. His nondenominational, nonsectarian approach has made his teaching equally relevant and helpful to people from all racial and religious backgrounds, and his teaching is estimated to have reached more than half the globe.

In 2002, he said, "It is my desire—and I believe the Lord's desire—that this ministry continue the work, which

God began through me over sixty years ago, until Jesus returns."

Derek Prince Ministries International continues to reach out to believers in over 140 countries with Derek's teaching, fulfilling the mandate to keep on "until Jesus returns." This is accomplished through the outreaches of more than thirty Derek Prince offices around the world, including primary work in Australia, Canada, China, France, Germany, the Netherlands, New Zealand, Norway, Russia, South Africa, Switzerland, the United Kingdom, and the United States. For current information about these and other worldwide locations, visit www.derekprince.org.